Faith A. Oyedepo

Single
With A
Difference

CONTENTS

DEDICATION

To:

David Oluwamakinde and Isaac Olugbemi, my beloved sons and ordained ministers of the gospel; Love Jesutobi and Joys Priscilla Abiola, my precious daughters.

Through exemplary lifestyle, you have demonstrated in practical terms, beyond any shadow of a doubt; the beauty of singleness. You are living proofs that it is possible to be single and positively different.

The truth shared in this book are gleaned mainly from your sound and distinguished lifestlye.

I am eternally grateful to God who has privileged me to be connected to you.

I love you with passion!

INTRODUCTION

To every thing there is a season ...

Ecclesiastes 3:1

Everything on earth is designed to function according to times and seasons. The sun, for instance, rises from the east at a certain time of the day and it must of a necessity change direction, heading towards the west as the day progresses and then sets ultimately as it is designed to do. No matter the weather condition, raining, cloudy, snowy or sunny, the sun never stays static. It keeps moving whether we can see it or not, until it arrives at its predetermined course in the West. In the same vein, every one born of a woman is designed to also live according to seasons of life.

Genesis 8:22 says:

While the earth remaineth, seedtime and harvest, and cold and heat, and summer and winter, and day and night shall not cease.

This clearly means that life is in phases and as long as the earth remains, different seasons of life shall

7

continually be in force. For you to fulfill destiny, you must have a good understanding of the season that you are in per time and possess a working knowledge of the demands, benefits and privileges of the same.

Whatever your age today, (whether twenty, twenty-five, thirty, forty or older), you cannot be that age forever; it can only be for the now! When the now is gone, that specific time of your life is gone forever and you can never recall it. That is why the above scriptures in Ecclesiastes 3:1 clearly state that to everything under the sun, including the single years, there is a time and a season.

Consider this for a moment: When a baby is born, he grows through childhood, adolescence, teenage years and single life; perhaps married life, mid-life, old age and then ultimately aged. The same is true of the family circle. You are first young and under the care and tutelage of your parents or guardians, then you are mature enough to begin to consider getting married, at which phase, you are referred to as being single. You get married, become a parent, a grand parent. Then after fulfilling the number of days, at a good old age, one of the spouses may translate to glory, then you become a widow or widower and back again to being single but now with an enlarged family tree.

God is awesome! Certainly, life is designed of God to be in phases and not static. Being single is just one of the seasons of life and unless effectively and maximally utilized, it fizzles away so fast and can never be recaptured. I have discovered interestingly, many singles spend this season of their lives as if it can be held down or stored away some place and relived when they so desire. They are so consumed with wanting to move to the next phase of life, which is being married that they fail to realise the beauty of their present phase. So, they miss out on the enormous plan and purpose of God for this season.

The Power Of Your Now

...behold, now is the accepted time; behold, now is the day of salvation.

2 Corinthians 6:2(b).

There is a time called the accepted time. That time is now! God believes in the now If you must live a life that is accepted to God, you must harness the power of your now. If you must enjoy the benefits of your tomorrow, your today must be effectively harnessed and utilized.

What you can do today, do not put off till tomorrow. What you can handle now that you are single, do not postpone till when you get married. It may be too late then. There is tremendous power available to you in your now!

What you do with your now, when you are still single, will ultimately determine what you will find in your future.

Your now is actually the womb that births your future, it is a pointer to your tomorrow. It is the seed that determines the kind of harvest you will reap later in your life.

Whatever you desire to find in your future life, this is the best time for you to set a pace for it, by the way you handle your single years. There is no time like the present, to start doing something worthwhile with your life. You know, you do not have a spare or duplicate life. You have only this one life to live. There is no return match in the game of life, so, you cannot afford to be careless with it. To be careless with life is to be consumed in it. So, handle it with care!

Many, who are older in life, end up regretting how they handled their single years. Their past years are gone and gone for eternity and cannot be re-captured and brought forward to be lived in the now! Please, do not make the same mistake, so you do not end your life in regret! Rise up and do something resourceful with your life now.

If your tomorrow must be great, the foundation for it has to be laid today. Your today is actually a product of how you handled your yesterday. Therefore, do not underestimate the power of your now.

God is a now God!

And God said unto Moses, I AM THAT I AM:

Exodus 3:14

He causes new things to spring forth on a now basis.

Behold, I will do a new thing; now it shall spring forth;
Isaiah 43: 19

Even faith, by which we live, is a now substance.

Now faith is the substance of things hoped for, the evidence of things not seen.
Hebrews 11:1

So, you really cannot make much of life without understanding the power of your now and effectively putting it to work.

You cannot afford to tiptoe through life! The best of life is yours for the taking – now! You can actually give your life its best now. Don't be careless or live life with a non-challant attitude. Get hold of your life and create a great future for yourself. Your single years are your best opportunity to lay a solid foundation for your future life, especially in marriage.

Wake up, and do something worthwhile with your life now!

Redeem The Time!

Life is actually timed! On the other hand, time is life. This explains the reason for the popular phrase "life time." Life is tied to time. In essence, it means the way you handle your time is a pointer to the way you handle your life. To waste time is to waste life and to invest time is to invest life.

Redeeming the time, because the days are evil.
Ephesians 5:16

The Word of God makes it clear in the above scripture that you are to redeem the time because the days are evil. In other words, unless the season of your single years is redeemed, it stands a chance of being caught up by the evil of the day.

Many young people spend time, hanging out with friends and stuff; very few actually invest it. It is very interesting to note that time can neither be stored nor held back. To be uniquely different as a single, you must redeem the time, investing rather than spending it.

To redeem time actually means to make it deliver its worth, honour and reputation to you. It means to take control of it, making the most of it. If you lose control of time, you lose control of your life. The truth is the best time to make this a lifestyle, is while you are still single.

The Millennial Generation

We live in a millennium where changes happen much faster than anyone can imagine. Take for instance, the Internet, which is up and running, at an unimaginable speed that helps you access news or information from all over the world in just a matter of seconds! Then think about the satellites above the earth, beaming what is happening in one part of the world to you, thousands of kilometers away. A fast generation! A pace - setting and innovative generation: where everything is moving at the speed of light. That is the generation we are in!

These are the last days and God has promised that He will pour out His Spirit upon all flesh. That explains why the events of life are beginning to run at the pace of the Spirit. Like the wind in John 3:8, no one can understand the fast pace of events anymore. Everything moves very fast.

In the midst of all these fast and wonderful changes, God has raised you as a single person, to be singled out for good, born in due season; born at such a time like this, a time of destiny; a time of purpose; a time when God's hand is mighty upon the earth! What a wonderful generation you belong to? What a wonderful time to be in this unique season of life: single with a difference!

You are unique as a single and that is why the Bible says concerning you in 1 Peter 2:9:

> *But ye are a chosen generation, a royal priesthood, an holy nation, a peculiar people; that ye should shew forth the praises of him who hath called you out of darkness into his marvelous light:*

Every phase of your development in life is designed

to deliver a specific contribution first to you as an individual, then to your immediate environment and ultimately to your world. God has specially crafted and sent you into the world at this time and has set you in this phase of your life and He is looking forward to seeing you succeed in this phase.

However, success is not accidental and it is not a gift. It is a product. Before you get any product, you need the correct raw materials, which must be processed appropriately.

Making my shoulders available!

Isaac Newton said, "If I have seen any further, it is by standing on the shoulders of those who have gone ahead of me."

Some time ago, while receiving a mandate for youths and singles, God said to me: *"Make your shoulders available to them."* I then asked Him, "How do I do this? He said, *"The things that you have heard, seen, looked upon, handled, experienced, taught and still teach and show your biological children, as well as, those who pass through your home about singleness and are producing undeniable evidences, teach and impart others"* (I John 1:1-3). Then He said to me, *"If they see brighter, they would live better lives, even as singles."* I have proof that it works! You will also become an evidence. I have a divine passion and I am therefore committed, to see you make the most of your single years!

So, in this most exciting work, I am going to be sharing some profound life changing principles with you from the word of God, which I consider as the raw materials you need to process, so as to arrive at your desired product. I have seen these work in my own life, those of my family, friends, co-workers, other Christians - single as well as those now married and I am confident they will produce results in your own very life as well.

The word of God is full of principles, which when appropriately processed, produce success in every area, including the single years. These principles though very simple, (remember that the Bible talks about the simplicity of the gospel), yet when put to work, enable you to make the most of your single years, thereby becoming positively different.

This book is designed to help every one that is single to appreciate the uniqueness, depth of opportunities and fun that God has loaded into this season of life to be enjoyed and taken advantage of.

You can be single, sound and positively different! Come along with me and let us explore how.

Chapter 1

THE BEAUTY OF SINGLENESS

...male and female created he them.

Genesis 1:27.

At creation, God first and foremost created two separate, distinct individuals: That is what singleness is all about. To be single means to be a whole, distinct and successful individual, capable of initiative and having the capacity to contribute to and enrich another person's life.

The *Oxford Advanced Learner's Dictionary* defines singles as "unmarried people, people who are not married and do not have a romantic relationship with somebody else. The state of singleness has also been described as a state of someone being unmarried, divorced, separated from the spouse, or widowed.

Singleness is beautiful!

Adam and Eve were created as singles before marriage was ever instituted (Genesis 2:7, 20-21). What a beautiful scenario it would have been for them. Imagine it for a moment. Adam was created, given an assignment to keep and dress the garden, name all of the creatures on earth. He was alone but not lonely. Life was beautiful as far as he was concerned. God only decided to create Eve as a help meet and not because Adam's life lacked meaning. Eve also was first created as a single individual, before she was brought to Adam.

Joseph, the earthly father of Jesus was a successful single, uniquely different from others in his days. He was so peculiar and positively different that God found him worthy for Jesus to come to the world through his lineage (Matthew 1:18-25). May God find you worthy as well!

Remember the four Hebrew boys: Daniel, Shadrach, Meshach and Abednego (Daniel 1:7). They were youths, singles who demonstrated the beauty of singleness in a grand style. They were so much outstanding that they were ten times better than all the others. Daniel in particular was said to be preferred above the presidents and princes, because an excellent spirit was in him (Daniel 6: 3). Isn't it amazing?

Timothy was Apostle Paul's son in the faith (1 Timothy 1: 1-2; 2 Timothy 1:1-2). As a young man, in his single years, he had an 'unfeigned faith.' He was one of Paul's missionary co-workers. He grew to become one of the greatest church leaders. History has it that he was the first Bishop in the New Testament. What an

THE BEAUTY OF SINGLENESS

accomplishment!

Think of the four daughters of Phillip the evangelist, who was one of the first seven Deacons of the church (Acts 21:8-9). These four ladies were in their single years. Interestingly, the bible specifically recorded that they were virgins and did prophesy. What a gift they were and still are to the body of Christ!

Titus, Lydia, Phoebe, Mary, Martha, Lazarus, among many others demonstrated the beauty of singleness by their outstanding accomplishments while single. You are the next on the line!

Then, consider Jesus our perfect example. Even though He was on a special divine assignment, He fulfilled His mission as a single.

Even when you come to think of it, everyone that is married was once single. Every career fellow, businessman or woman, parent, etc was once or is still single. Little wonder then, that the single years are the foundation for a glorious and secure future.

I cannot emphasize enough the importance of this stage of life in your quest for an eventual successful future as well as married life. The more auspicious you are as a single, the better your chances of thriving in your future life and marriage subsequently.

To be single is to be whole!

To be single is to be whole, outstanding, unique,

separate and positively different! God is interested in your wholeness. To be whole, you must discover who you are in the context of God's word. You must act on your discoveries from the word. You must learn the art of instant forgiveness, knowing fully well that hatred hurts the hater more than the hated. And of course, you must be driven by the passion of wanting to add value to people's lives.

That you are single now does not mean that you are a sub-standard or incomplete being. No, never entertain such feeling or thought! In fact, let me state categorically here that being single is not a curse neither is it a disease. It is a blessing, a plus, not a minus, an addition, not a subtraction. It is not weird to be single and is certainly not an evil thing. It is simply a phase of life that holds undeniable benefits for those who utilize it.

God is not an unrighteous God and He certainly is no respecter of persons. What He does for one, He is willing, ready, and able to do for another. He is not more righteous to one as to favour him than He is to another. He is rich unto all that call upon His name- and that includes you! He knows your phase per time and He has not forgotten you.

Don't live your single years wondering if God has forgotten you or whether you are under a curse. No! Never! God is too faithful to fail, He is dependable, and He is more than enough - I am a living proof!

Life, as you know, is in phases and singleness is a phase that everyone must of necessity pass through in the journey of life: whether as a married person, a eunuch, a celibate, a career person or whatever choice you make. Every stage or phase in life has its inherent benefits, which should be harnessed and singleness is no exception. May you enjoy the added benefit inherent in the single years!

Singleness is a phase of life that you must pass through and the faster you are able to maximise the season and pass the examinations of that phase of life, the faster you move on to the next phase of your life.

When I was single, there were some of my colleagues whose only focus in life was marriage. Nothing else had meaning or attracted them except marital issues. Most of them don't have much to show for it even now! This is obviously misplaced priority. Life is much more than that. It is very important for you to get your bearings right in life, now that you are still single.

As you go through this material, you will be amazed to see that the single years is a colourful and beautiful season, loaded with abundant benefits and opportunities. So, rather than whiling away time, or sitting down bemoaning your situation; wishing, desiring and devising means to get out of singleness, you can productively engage this season to deliver all that it holds for you before it's over.

Benefits Of Singleness

It Helps You To Draw Near To God

The benefits of the single years cut across the three dimensions of your life – spirit, soul and body. It takes an effective harnessing of these three dimensions to enjoy maximally the benefits of the single years.

The Bible in Ecclesiastes 12:1 says:

> *Remember now thy Creator in the days of thy youth, while the evil days come not, nor the years draw nigh, when thou shalt say, I have no pleasure in them;*

The days of your youth in the above scripture means your single years. Those years are the most effective time to be actively engaged in the pursuit and service of your creator. Man was created for only one purpose - to bring God pleasure.

> *Thou art worthy, O Lord, to receive glory and honour and power: for thou hast created all things, and for thy pleasure they are and were created.*
>
> Revelation 4:11

Therefore, you must be committed to doing just that. You cannot live a sound life and be positively different while single without the help of God. The foundation for a great spiritual life is usually laid in the single years of one's life. This cannot be achieved in the energy of the flesh. Remember that without God, all your efforts in life amount to nothing (John 15: 5). Your only sure foundation for a secure future is God.

While yet single, you must understand and appreciate the fact that God seeks an intimate relationship with you. Concerning you, He says in James. 4:8

Draw nigh to God, and he will draw nigh to you. Cleanse your hands, ye sinners; and purify your hearts, ye double minded.

Your closeness to God while you are still single is the bedrock of your future life, the security of your destiny. No other relationship can equal or replace the one with God. You know what? Any human will fail you, but God cannot! I can tell you this with every sense of responsibility – God is too faithful to fail!

Draw near to God! It is for your good, not God's. God is not dependent on you; rather you are dependent on Him. When you draw near to God, He will in turn draw near to you. Your closeness to God has to be initiated by you. Yes, I can hear someone say "How do you mean? I am a Christian, I am born again and I even speak in tongues! Well, thank God for your life. But no matter how near you are to God right now, you can draw nearer still.

SINGLE WITH A DIFFERENCE

Personally, I have found out that the closer you walk with God, the more you see the need to draw closer yet. I love the song of one great songwriter that says, *"Just a closer walk with you, grant it Jesus this is my plea…"*

The truth is, your relationship with God will reflect in your relationship with man. How you treat people is a pointer to how you treat God. There are some singles that chase marriage as a dog chasing a rabbit, especially those who are of marriageable age. For you who are in the kingdom, it ought not to be so. To anybody in this class I say, relax!

It should not be marriage at all cost. Remember that Adam was put to a deep sleep before the wife manifested (Genesis 2: 21-22). Pursue, chase God; not marriage and every other thing shall be added unto you, including a glorious marriage. Make God your focus in life, not marriage.

Proverbs 18:21 says:

Whosoever findeth a wife findeth a good thing, and obtaineth favour of the LORD.

'Find' in the above scripture means, 'to discover along the way.' So, when you are in a close relationship with God, along the way you will miraculously discover your marriage partner. Don't join those who attend meetings and gatherings primarily in search of a marriage partner;

searching, matching and comparing potential candidates.

Are you due for marriage? Please be aware that God has not forgotten you! God cannot mismanage your life. Stop searching for a marriage partner at all cost. Make Jesus your Lord, your Boss and be deeply committed to Him. This is the excellent foundation for your future.

Or, do you feel imprisoned by circumstances that seem to be beyond your control? Don't be anxious. Do not panic. Don't lose hope. Why? I seem to hear you ask. You know what? I can assure you that it will work out for your good, not against you. You don't know what God has in store for you – no matter your age! You know what? God is still in the business of divine connections!

This word of assurance in Romans 8:28 is for you. Receive it today. It says:

> **And we know that all things work together for good to them that love God, to them who are the called according to his purpose.**

"But how do I draw near to God?" you may ask. Good question.

First, engage in constant, deep study of the word of God. You cannot draw close to God without deep Word study. 2 Timothy 2:15 says:

> **Study to shew thyself approved unto God, a workman that needeth not to be ashamed, rightly**

dividing the word of truth.

Real Word study involves attentive scrutiny and research. Invest quality time in searching the scriptures. Read different versions of the bible especially on specific issues that affect you. Make use of your concordance as well as a dictionary.

While you are still single is the best time to develop this. When it is time to make a choice in marriage, your deep word study life helps you choose correctly, thereby delivering you from wolves in sheep's clothing. If you do not practise this when you are single, it will be much more difficult if not impossible for you later in life.

I gave my life to Christ and got born again as a teenager. Ever since then, by the help of God, I have maintained a lifestyle of daily, constant, regular Word study. Presently, there are certain books, chapters and portions of the bible that I study daily. This practice has helped me in no small measure to build a close relationship with God. This does not mean that once in a while I don't miss my daily time of Word study, but it is very rare. When brothers started approaching me on the issue of marriage when I was single, it was easy for me to be guided by God and not be misled by the mixed multitude.

Remember Romans 8:6 which says:

For to be carnally minded is death; but to be spiritually minded is life and peace.

And John. 6:63,

...the words that I speak unto you, they are spirit, and they are life.

When the word of God dwells richly in you, your relationship with Him is enriched and this in turn affects every area of your life positively.

Second, be armed with the weapon of prayer. The Word says in Luke 18:1,

...men ought always to pray, and not to faint:

To pray means to commune with God. Without any doubt, communication strengthens relationship. Prayer becomes most refreshing and fulfilling, when you keep it practical and simple. Of course, it must come from the heart and must be prayed in faith.

For me, from when I was single, there was nothing too small or too big to pray about. I can tell you this – it works! It is not how long you pray but how well. Prayer can be effectively prayed in small segments of time: day or night, in private or public. One of the most treasured times of my life is when I am communing with my father in heaven in prayer. Oh, it is sweet and God answers prayers! I am a living proof and a product of answered prayer.

Third, attend fellowship regularly. Let it become a part and parcel of your life. Attend Christian gatherings. Meet with other believers of like minds and share fellowship together.

Hebrews 10:25 says:

Not forsaking the assembling of ourselves together, as the manner of some is; but exhorting one another: and so much the more, as ye see the day approaching.

Don't just be a Christian who go to church only on Sundays. Be not deceived, what you sow determines what you reap. When I was in high school as a young girl, five of us girls formed a group and we always had times of prayer, word study and fellowship. Those days, I believe were a kind of spiritual deposit into the future, from where I am still drawing dividends today after many years. Let me ask you this question. How regular are you in fellowship?

It Is The Prime Time Of Life

Another cardinal benefit of the single years is that it is the prime time of life. I strongly believe that it is in recognition of this that the bible says in Ecclesiastes 12:1,

Remember now thy Creator in the days of thy youth, while the evil days come not, nor the years draw nigh, when thou shalt say, I have no pleasure in them;

And 1 Timothy 4:12 says:

Let no man despise thy youth; but be thou an example of the believers, in word, in conversation, in charity, in spirit, in faith, in purity.

Unusual strength is one of the characteristics of this prime time of life. While single, you feel you can conquer the whole world. Your strength seems to be at the peak. You become very adventurous. This explains why youths and singles are known for unusual strength.

It is the best time for self-discovery as well as your mission on earth. It is a time to find out, where you actually belong in life. Many people in life get lost in the shadow of others, living as carbon copies when in actual fact they are created original. This is the best time to develop your own personality.

To discover who you are, it must begin with an understanding of the fact that you are uniquely valuable. You have the opportunity to accomplish personal goals, pursue a variety of interests and work out personal problems. By so doing, you acquire and develop skills that might become an asset to you in future. You are able to take decisions and accept responsibility for them. This decisions and your willinness to take responsibility in turn make for maturity. Remember that maturity comes by reason of adequate correct exercise (Hebrews 5:14).

29

In his single years, before I met my husband, he developed special interest in writing articles and giving to some of his seniors then to proof read and mark for him. Even though most of those articles were not published then, I believe that the experience has helped his writing ministry in no small measure today.

Mobility

Mobility is one other benefit of singleness. There is movement not only of the physical body, but also the mobility of time, money and decision. For instance, singleness permits greater freedom to respond to new job opportunities. This is because only personal consideration is required before such movements. Even when you are to make trips, movement is easier. Your speed is enhanced because you require lesser time to plan and execute your plans.

Financially, you enjoy cost effectiveness because lesser money is spent since you are the only one involved. It is the best time to learn and practice the principles for effective money handling. Develop the required strategies to make money your servant, not your master.

Freedom To Serve The Lord Without Distraction

While single, distractions are limited and this enhances your relationship with God and service in the kingdom. The Bible says in 1 Corinthians 7:32 & 35:

> *But I would have you without carefulness. He that is unmarried careth for the things that belong to the Lord, how he may please the Lord :*
>
> *And this I speak for your own profit; not that I may cast a snare upon you, but for that which is comely, and that ye may attend upon the Lord without distraction.*

Involvement in Christian activity groups, fasting, prayer, fellowship, word study, helps ministry, and many others, is one of the benefits of your single years. While single, I was involved in various Christian activity groups such as the choir, drama, visitation, prayer and bible study outline development groups at different times and places. I was able to develop the ability to serve God in the helps ministry as an intercessor. I learnt to engage in long fasting periods coupled with prayer and word study, which is an asset today to me. This has created in me a strong desire and passion to want to make contribution to mankind in every small way possible. You know what? Some of those marathon fasting I did then, I would not dare them now at this time anymore. Wow!

Before we got married, my husband was involved in several Christian activity groups and long term prayer and fasting. Some of those days he would go to the top of the mountain to wait on the Lord, days and night, come rain or sunshine. He would not get involved in some of those stuff at this time of his life anymore, at least not at that frequency. This is because the wisest time to do such was then, which has come and gone. Thank God he responded at the right time.

Please understand that I am not saying that you cannot serve God except you are single. The truth is, if you cannot do so while single, it will be much more difficult when married. And again, there is time for everything under the sun (Ecclesiastes 3:1). There are some kind and degree of kingdom involvement that wisdom demands should be maximized while single. You have a golden opportunity now that you are still single. Take advantage of it. You need to take action now before it is too late.

Freedom From Marital Responsibilities And Concerns

You are free from marital responsibilities and concerns when you are single. Marriage comes with attendant responsibilities. The married cares for how to please God as well as his or her spouse (I Corinthians 7:33-34). As singles, you don't have to please or pick up after someone, tolerate another's moodiness, nagging or anger. You do not have to deal with another's personal habits that has the potential to create tension in marriage such as squeezing of the toothpaste in the middle of the tube!

You are not responsible for another's careless behavior as in the case of Abigail (1 Samuel 25: 1- 34). But for her timely intervention in wisdom, she and her entire household would have perished under David's anger engineered by Nabal her husband. You do not even have to deal with scars from a broken marriage or divorce.

Do not spend your single years wishing and waiting to be married. Instead, make it count so that you would be able to make impact that will be remembered for generations after you. You shall not end your journey in disgrace!

Chapter 2

MAKE YOUR FOUNDATION SURE

If the foundations be destroyed, what can the righteous do?

Psalms 11:3

Many years ago, we lived in a city where an estate comprising of many houses were built by the government. Unfortunately, after the buildings were completed, it was discovered that there was a fundamental error at the foundation. So, all the buildings in the whole estate were abandoned and later completely demolished, as they were not habitable. I leant a great lesson from that incidence that has stayed with me ever since.

Foundation is everything! Nothing can adequately substitute the need for a solid foundation. A building with a faulty foundation is a dangerous one to live in; it is usually evidenced by cracks all over. No reinforcement can adequately repair the cracks. The foundation of a house is what determines how stable, strong and lasting the building will be. Every building with a faulty foundation must necessarily, be pulled down or it will collapse of its own accord like a pack of cards, with time.

It is very clear from the word of God and particularly from the above scripture that there is nothing anyone can do, not even the righteous, if the foundations be destroyed. As it is with the foundation, so it goes with the building. A faulty foundation makes every other part of the building faulty.

Your single years are actually the foundation years of your life and destiny. If you do not lay a solid foundation for your life while single, the future cannot be guaranteed. Your destiny shall not collapse!

The quality of success you will ever attain in life and destiny, hinges on the quality of the foundation you lay in your single years. That is what the single years of your life are designed for. You cannot experience a glorious future, without paying attention to your foundation in your single years. Now that you are still single, may I ask you this all important question – What kind of foundation are you laying for your future?

If, for instance, as a teenager you could not concentrate enough to study and pass your examinations, it will be foolhardy for you to imagine that after marriage and five children, all below ten years of age and all demanding your attention as a mother, you can now choose to study and pass that same examination. It will be near impossible.

The word 'foundation' actually means 'the solid underground base for something.' *The Oxford Advanced Learner's Dictionary* defines 'foundation' as principles, ideas and facts on which something is based; a basis for something.

There are certain profound principles that you must have a firm grip of in your quest for ensuring a solid foundation while single. Let's examine some of them closely.

Get connected and committed to your creator

The foundation for a secure life and destiny is first and foremost in your connection and commitment to God, the author of life and creator of all living.

John 15:5 says:

> *I am the vine, ye are the branches: He that abideth in me, and I in him, the same bringeth forth much fruit: for without me ye can do nothing.*

The foundation for a secure life and destiny is in your personal relationship with God. He is the one who founded the whole earth including your destiny. So, you need a personal encounter with Him. The quality of your relationship with the Almighty God, will affect and determine the quality of life you will enjoy. How vital and strong the quality of your relationship with God is, will determine the quality and strength of your ultimate destiny.

God is the only source of true and lasting life. When you let God into the ship of your life and destiny, it can never sink. As a single person, a good understanding of this will help you walk through life with confidence. It is very important for you to understand that God is the only source of true joy, contentment and satisfaction in life, not your parents, friends, colleagues or spouse.

From the above scripture, it is evident that for your life to be fruitful, you cannot do away with the God factor. He is the only one that can help you actualize your desired end. He must be the foundation upon which your future must be built. The single years of your life, make up the period when you learn the virtues that will help you lay a solid foundation in God.

Recognize and give God His rightful place in your life. Get connected and committed! Commitment can be likened to a man's spinal cord. Without it, your life and destiny may suffer a nervous breakdown. For lack of commitment, many destinies have crashed! If you are genuinely and scripturally committed to God, you will be committed to the success of your destiny.

Several years ago, before we got married, my husband wrote a paper he titled **"Sailing Under Sealed Orders."** It was a demonstration of his unwavering commitment to God. I have reproduced a copy of it here verbatim. My sincere desire, prayer and belief is that it ministers to you and set you on the right path of destiny. Read it over and again, meditate on it and act accordingly.

SAILING UNDER SEALED ORDERS

12/9/76

Where, I do not know!

When, I cannot say!

Why, is not my business and How, must not concern me, but It is mine to accept from Him the sealed orders containing His blueprint for my life, and to open and read them just when and just as much as a time as He wills.

It is saying an eternal "Yes" to God. And eternal "No" to self.

"Lord, what will thou have me to do? Where will thou have me to go?

Having definitely relingquished all claims I deliberately turn my back on everything. Thus I renounce all that I am and have.

It's no longer mine but God's.

Henceforth, He has the absolute right to do what he like with it, and if at any time he should call upon me to literally forsake what I have renounced I must not even murmur or complain.

He must be Lord of all, or not Lord at all.

I particularly love the last statement in the write up: "Christ must be Lord of all, or not Lord at all." That is why I am not surprised at where God has brought him and the ministry today.

Commitment is what drives a vision. Until you are committed to what you are created for on the earth, you will never truly realise it. Like the hub of a bicycle that holds the spooks together, so is commitment to the realisation of your destiny. Prayer and fasting cannot take the place of commitment. It takes a solid foundation of commitment to God, to be able to learn commitment to any other thing you desire to become in future.

Even if your only purpose for living in your single years is to be married, yet, the level of your commitment to the success of your marriage will be determined by the level of commitment to God that you have learnt in your years as a single person. The importance of the God factor in your quest for laying a solid foundation for your life cannot be over-emphasized!

Maximize Your Single Days

Many singles have a problem knowing what to do with their lives while waiting for marriage or a glorious future. All that most young men and women do is to fast, pray and believe God for a spouse. Then, they soon start counting days and years; giving ultimatum to God. In such a state of anxiety, they begin to think that God is slow and that they are getting too old for marriage. But you can maximise your single years and make them exciting, purposeful, and full of fun.

Concerning you, the word of God says:

> *For I know the plans I have for you," says the Lord.*
> *"They are plans for good and not for evil, to give*
> *you a future and a hope.*
>
> Jeremiah 29:11 (TLB)

God has good plans for your single days, as a single man or woman; not just for when you are married. But most individuals because of their ignorance of God's plan for them in this period, do not make the best use of it. They spend so much time anxiously wondering when they will meet their spouse. If you desire a good future, you are the one to work it out and this takes hard work; which is the essential trait that can enhance your worth and prospects in life.

Invest In Your Life As A Person

The best time for you to start investing into your life is while you are still single. This should affect every area of your life – spiritual, mental, emotional and physical. Now let's look at each of these areas briefly.

Spiritually

The single years are the best period to get acquainted

with God. Get to know Him and let Him get to know you. Take time out in word study and meditation, unhindered by family responsibilities. Search the scriptures and other relevant materials so as to learn what you are expected to do, so as to make happen what you desire to make of your life.

Grow in grace and draw closer to God daily by communing with Him in prayer. As you do this, you will sharpen your discernment and also be fervent enough to be able to build a God - honouring home tomorrow. Marriage, by its very nature involves a lot of giving and your spiritual stamina will contribute, in no small measure, to your ability to build wisely.

Serve the Lord unreservedly. You can serve the Lord unreservedly during your single days with unbroken focus. God's word in Matthew 6:33 points out what your focus should be, if you want to enjoy all other things life and salvation have to offer.

> *But seek ye first the kingdom of God, and his righteousness; and all these things shall be added unto you.*

If your purpose for living does not include serving the Lord, then you do not have a right purpose for living. Serving the lord prevents aimless wondering.

There are many areas in which you can render service

to the Lord. Join service groups. Refuse to be idle, don't be a bench warmer in church. Be actively and productively involved. Find a need and fill it. Be dedicated in the service of the Lord.

Mentally

Build yourself up mentally. Be the best you can and enhance your worth. Develop skills. Develop yourself greatly in your chosen field of endeavor or career. Water, they say, seeks its own level. Your single days are an opportunity to exhibit the qualities you want in your future.

Cultivate the winning attitudes that will be relevant for the future you desire. For instance, if someday you desire to be a big time corporate executive, your single years, are the time to cultivate the habits required for that position. Read relevant books. Task your brain. Make it sweat. Learn the art of thinking aright.

Your mental faculty is situated in the mind. Now that you are born again, remember that 2 Corinthians 2:16(b) says:

But we have the mind of Christ.

Until you develop your mind, your world will never mind you! So, you have a responsibility to keep renewing your mind and developing it through adequate relevant exercises. Engage it productively (Ephesians 4:23).

Learn as much as you can about marriage from credible sources, not from negative examples around you. Study the Bible, the primary text on the subject of marriage. Study relevant materials such as books, tapes, magazines, etc. by those with not just knowledge of the subject but, also proven testimonies in their marriages. The main difference between a marriage that is working and the one that is not, is knowledge (Daniel 11:32; 1 Peter 3:7). Study and understand God's provisions for the family, how to run a home, how to relate with in-laws, etc, and also study the biographies of successful couples.

Go to school, acquire relevant knowledge and broaden your knowledge base. Create and embrace opportunities to better yourself, so that you will be an asset tomorrow and not a liability.

Emotionally

Emotionally, develop yourself and your capacity to accommodate other people, unconditionally, for the rest of your life. Life is all about giving, not just receiving. God created us with emotions. Therefore, you need to learn in your single days, how to be tolerant and to handle issues with your emotions under control. You must learn how not to be controlled by your emotions. You should control them.

Learn to forgive. Forgive yourself and others

(Matthew 6:12). Forgive those who have done you evil – knowingly or unknowingly. You cannot undo the past but you can recover it. Don't get into what can bring you regret. Don't forget that hatred is poisonous; flee it.

In the same vein, beware of anger! Remember these words.

Be slow to anger (Nehemiah 9:17).

Put off anger, wrath, malice (Colossians 3:8).

Anger resteth in the bosom of fools (Ecclesistes 7:9).

Grievous words stir up anger (Proverbs 15:1).

Fear, anxiety and the like all have a lot to do with the mind. You must learn to handle them effectively, while you are still single. Some singles have the fear of the unknown. They are anxious about the future and thereby lose control of the present.

Physically

Keep yourself fit physically.

> **I beseech you therefore, brethren, by the mercies of God, that ye present your bodies a living sacrifice, holy, acceptable unto God, which is your reasonable service.**
>
> Romans 12:1

You have a duty to present your body unto God as a living and acceptable sacrifice. Your body is the temple of God (1 Corinthians 6:19-20). Keep it holy, free from every form of contaminants – spiritually and physically. Whatever does not glorify God should not be allowed in your body. Whatever defiles the body should be done away with. Sin – especially sexual sin should not be allowed (Romans 6:14).

Sexual sin, you must understand carries untold consequences along with it. Apart from inviting God's wrath, there are about thirty-nine sexually transmitted diseases that have been identified with it to date. Sexual sin is a silent killer; flee it!

Also, as a part of investing into your life physically, you need to get involved in household chores that will become assets to you in future. For example, cleanliness, it is said, is next to godliness. While single, male or female; keep your environment clean. Wash, iron, sweep, mow, decorate, organize your closet and arrange your bookshelves: put some order into your life! These are investments that you will appreciate as long as you live.

As a lady, learn how to keep the house, cook and generally manage a home. As a man, learn how to be responsible and to take care of someone else apart from yourself. It will interest you to know that I have my personal cookbook, even now. This is one of the things I have developed over the years. So now, every professional cook that works in my home, has no choice but to respect my authority in that area.

Understand Your Uniqueness

To be able to lay a solid foundation for your life, you need a good understanding of your uniqueness. 1 Peter 2:9 says:

But ye are a chosen generation, a royal priesthood, an holy nation, a peculiar people; that ye should shew forth the praises of him who hath called you out of darkness into his marvelous light;

A good understanding of your uniqueness will help you to make the most out of life and be a greater blessing to others. There is only one of your kind on planet earth, sent here for a definite purpose. Never be deceived to want to be someone else. You are just original! Accept your originality and make the most of it.

Every thing about God is unique; He excels in varieties. In creating the human race, there are no two persons who are exactly alike. Even men and women are unique in their own different make up. One star is different from another in glory, the word of God says.

There is one glory of the sun, and another glory of the moon, and another glory of the stars: for one star differeth from another star in glory.

1 Corinthians 15:41

47

God's word also says:

God created man in his own image, in the image of God created he him; male and female created he them.

Genesis 1:27

It is clearly stated in the above scriptures that, the man and woman are unique right from creation. He created them male and female. It is important for you to appreciate the differences between the male and female genders of God's creation. Whether you are a man or woman, you are not an after-thought of God's creation; so, do not feel inferior about your gender. No matter your gender, God has a purpose for creating you the way you are. God equally has a purpose for making you the person you are; so, get excited because you are created to suit your purpose.

For God to fulfill His eternal purposes, He used two physical forms, called male and female, to express the one entity of man. From the scriptures you will observe that when God speaks to humanity, He uses the term 'man' (Numbers 23:19; Job. 33:12; Psalms 104:23; Proverbs 12:2, Matthew 6:24). He doesn't address the male or female unless He is talking to individuals (Genesis 2:25). God deals with the 'man' inside us – the inner man, because God is a spirit and true worshipers must worship him in spirit and in truth (John 4:24). It is important for you to know that we worship God with our spirits, not with our gender.

Some people have problems with this fact because they believe that being "different" means being either inferior or superior. Never equate being different to being less. Man and woman are both equal in the sense that they were both created in the image of God and their differences are only functional. Their differences are necessary because of their purposes. Men and women, the male and female genders of God's creation are meant to complement each other, not to compete with each other.

When God made the woman and presented her to Adam, he said,

"This is now... bone of my bones." In other words, he was saying, "This person is exactly like me in structure."

Secondly, he said, *"This is now ... flesh of my flesh"* (Genesis 2:23)

What Adam was saying, I believe is "She is exactly like me in all her physical qualities and in all of her emotional and psychological ability." Adam saw no differences. "We are the same, we are equal," he said.

So, never look down on anyone on the gender basis anymore! Each one is unique, including you!

Chapter 3

LOCATE THE REASON FOR YOUR EXISTENCE

Before I formed thee in the belly I knew thee; and before thou camest forth out of the womb I sanctified thee, and I ordained thee a prophet unto the nations.

Jeremiah 1:5

There is a reason for your existence. Before you were formed in your mother's womb, God knew you and set you aside for something specific. That specific thing that you have been set aside for is the reason for your existence. You are not an after-thought or a biological accident, the circumstance surrounding your birth notwithstanding. Even if you were born out of wedlock, you did not just happen or appear on this earth by mistake. You were made. This explains why Psalms 100:3 says:

Know ye that the Lord he is God: it is he that hath made us, and not we ourselves; we are his people, and the sheep of his pasture.

God, your manufacturer deliberately packaged you and sent you here for a specific reason. You are a high-tech product, packaged to perform certain defined functions. You exist for a definite reason. This reason is not for you to determine, it was already pre-determined by God before your existence.

It is a known fact that every product delivers its best when used according to the manufacturer's design. So also, you cannot live a distinguished and outstanding life, until you locate the reason for your existence and abide in it. There is a particular course to which you have been separated. You can only be positively different and stand out when you are in the center of God's assignment for you on the earth.

According to the *Cambridge Advanced Learner's Dictionary*, the word *'locate'* means to find or discover. The word *'exist'* means to be, to be real, to live. So, to locate the reason for your existence means to find or discover the reason why you live. God determined it but you have to discover it. So, even though there is a reason for your existence, it is your responsibility to find it out. You have been assigned to accomplish a particular task or mission. Locate it, abide in it and pursue it with all excitement; you will definitely live a positively different life!

Paul the Apostle lived an outstanding life because he

discovered this truth. He knew he was separated unto something right from his mother's womb. He located it and lived for it. Galatians 1:15 says:

> **But when it pleased God, who separated me from my mother's womb, and called me by his grace,**

So also, Joseph, Gideon, Esther, Jeremiah, Peter and indeed everyone who lived an outstanding life, including Jesus, did so on the basis of their discovery of the reason for their existence (1 John. 3: 8). However, you must understand that locating the reason for your existence is a personal, non-transferable responsibility. It is the master key to a life of distinction. Until you locate this reason why you exist, you are a disaster going somewhere to happen!

May I tell you this with all sense of responsibility - Now that you are still single is the best time to find out the reason for your existence! To miss this reason is to live in misery. I had always known, from my youth that I was going to be involved in ministry work; though I never knew the magnitude. The mandate for this ministry was delivered to my husband the visioner before we got married, while he was still single. The silver jubilee marking the first 25 years of the ministry was celebrated in May, 2006. It is amazing, what God has done! But, it all began during the single years.

Let me ask you this question – What is the reason for your existence on earth? This is the only way for you to find bearing for your life. May you locate it on time and live solely for it. You shall not be a disappointment to destiny!

But how can I locate this singular reason for which I exist? You may ask. Well, let me share the following hints with you. Let's examine three of the avenues here. I can guarantee they will be very useful in giving you a clue.

Go directly to God, your manufacturer

One major way you can locate the reason for your existence is by enquiry. Enquiry is what leads to discovery (Habakkuk 2:1-3). Ask God, your manufacturer. The best way to know what a product was made for is by consulting the manufacturer. Since God is your manufacturer, He has first hand information on what you have been separated unto before you ever existed. Matthew 7:7–8 says:

> *Ask, and it shall be given you; seek, and ye shall find; knock, and it shall be opened unto you: For everyone that asketh receiveth; ...*

And Jeremiah 29:13 says:

> *And ye shall seek me, and find me, when ye shall search for me with all your heart.*

Pray to God from the depth of your heart, with meekness (Psalms 25:9). Without meekness, this is an impossible task. Your prayer should be from a sincere heart that is willing to know, not a heart that is already made up and concluded on what to do. Consult the manufacturer's manual, the Bible; it contains God's blueprint for your life. God's reason for your existence will never be contrary to His word.

One of the most frequent and fervent prayers, I still remember very clearly that I ever prayed, especially in my single years, was along this line. It's not a surprise today where God has taken me. He will do the same thing for you. So, ask God in prayer and He is eager to show you where you belong. I am a living proof that it works!

Look inwards!

Conduct an internal search. This is another major way of locating the reason for existence. Take an inventory of your life. There is something within you that will give you a clue to where you belong. But be true to yourself. Remember that no one knows the things in a man except the spirit within him. Look inward for one or a combination of two or more of the following; it may be a pointer to your reason for existence.

Talents:

Every one has talents, gifts and endowments from

God, but you need to look inwards to discover them. King David enjoyed leading sheep, so he qualified to lead men. God gives gifts according to man's several abilities. There is no un-talented person on earth. Matthew 25:15 says:

> *And unto one he gave five talents, to another two, and to another one; to every man according to his several ability; and straightway took his journey.*

What productive thing do you have the ability to do without stress or imitations? It flows out of you naturally with delight. It is put there by God to occupy you till He comes (Luke 19:13). For me, writing is one of such. As I work on this material right now, I have been on this desk all night for about six straight hours tirelessly and I tell you its flowing! This is aside from several other such times already invested into this work.

Passion:

Where is your passion? There is something that you are usually very passionate about. What gives you boundless enthusiasm? You seem to have supernatural energy in pursuing such task. You are highly emotional about it. You get emotionally caught up in your actions and reactions concerning it. Locate it; it may be a pointer to your assignment on earth.

Nehemiah had unquenchable passion for the afflicted

in Jerusalem and the broken walls of the city. He pursued it and he was made (Nehemiah 2:1-20). In verse 3, Nehemiah said to the king:

> *...why should not my countenance be sad, when the city, the place of my fathers' sepulchers, lieth waste, and the gates thereof are consumed with fire?*

The renowned Mother Theresa was not known to have heard a voice from heaven, but she had a passion for the helpless lepers and she emerged one of the few that have influenced the world. Personally, I have a strong passion for ministering to singles, women, and families.

Skill:

Your skill is the proficiency, facility or dexterity that you have acquired or developed through training or experience over a period of time. David acquired skill through his experience with the lion and the bear. With this, he was able to overcome Goliath and eventually ascended the throne as king (1 Samuel 17).

What have you been trained to do? Skill could be acquired through training. Over the years, I have been able to improve my teaching and writing skill with the help of God.

Honest opinions:

What are people's honest opinions about you? What are your areas of positive impact on people? However, you must be very careful so as to avoid flatteries and deceit from people. Remember that the heart of man is deep and desperately wicked! Don't keep seeking people's approval and commendations. Never allow commendations from people create pride in you. Remain humble in your own eyes. I am personally very cautious about this.

At God's instance:

This is another way by which you can discover the reason for your existence. God, in His omnipotence and infinite mercy may choose to reveal to you your mission on earth, without your even asking Him for it. God is awesome! This was the case with Gideon in Judges. 6:11- 40. Verse 14 says:

> **And the Lord looked upon him, and said, Go in this thy might, and thou shalt save Israel from the hand of the Midianites: have not I sent thee?**

Abraham's experience was similar. Genesis. 12:1 says:

> **Now the LORD had said unto Abram, Get thee out of thy country, and from thy kindred, and from thy father's house, unto a land that I will shew thee:**

Abraham's life is still speaking today. It will interest you to note that the mandate of our ministry was also delivered after this order. God appeared to my husband, the visioner, as he shared the vision, in an 18-hour long encounter where the mandate was delivered. He was not particularly asking concerning this at this point in time. This happened while he was still single. Today, the effect of this mission all over the world cannot be denied. God will reveal Himself to you also!

As I close this chapter, let me make this very clear to you, that you are the primary beneficiary if you locate your reason for existence and abide in it. Remember, life without bearing is a burden! God has nothing to lose. Some of the benefits you stand to gain include, but are not limited to the following:

Meaningful living:

The discovery of the reason for your existence is what gives meaning to life. Finding what you are created to do and doing it, will turn you into a single with value and positive distinction. It gives fulfillment and makes accomplishment a reality. Many in life are not fulfilled because they have not yet discovered their mission on earth. Remember, life is a journey and only those with a definite destination ever get there. With the many hours invested into putting this material together, I enjoy a tremendous amount of fulfillment that money cannot buy! You will get there!

Focus

When you know where you are going, it automatically

keeps you focused. You are able to easily fight distraction. You do not easily fall a victim of being a jack of all trade, master of none. The potentials within you find expression and you begin to break every limitation arrayed against you. Your face is set like a flint, until you arrive at your expected end.

Energy

You enjoy a continuous supply of energy when you are pursuing the mission for which you exist. The energy and vigour to accomplish your given task, is usually available. When a man is easily tired on an assignment or task, it may be a sign that he is on the wrong track in life. How is your energy level, doing what you are doing right now?

Eradication of Waste

When you are committed to the pursuit of your God-given goals, you live a waste-free life. Waste of time, manpower and resources; to name a few are completely eradicated. I personally enjoy these in my own life and you can, too.

Chapter 4

SECURING YOUR FUTURE

For I know the thoughts that I think toward you, says the LORD, thoughts of peace and not of evil, to give you a future and a hope.

Jeremiah 29:11 (NKJ)

God has planned a glorious future for you. He so much loves you that He thinks thoughts of peace concerning you, ever desiring the establishment of this glorious future. What a joy, that even while you are still single, God is thinking about you! This is absolutely awesome! Whatever your situation or circumstance right now, you must settle it in your heart that the future God has planned for you is a glorious one. I rejoice with you!

However, glorious as it may be, for this future to become a reality, it has to be built and secured. Else it may remain a daydream that may never see the light of day or gets fulfilled.

From the *American Heritage Dictionary* and *the Oxford*

Advanced Learners Dictionary, the word *'secure'* means to free something from the risk of loss, danger or attack. Not likely to fail or give away; stable, certain, guaranteed. Firmly fastened, fixed, safe, and protected.

So, for your glorious future not to fail, give away or suffer the risk of loss, you have a part to play and now that you are still single is the best time to begin that.

Abraham Lincoln, US President (1861-5) said:

> *"The best thing about the future is that it only comes one day at a time."*

Inevitably, the future will soon be upon you! Tomorrow will soon be today this is the best time to face your future.

Accept Responsibility, Partner with God!

A wise man has said 'Responsibility is the price for greatness.' This is very true. It is your responsibility to secure your future! It won't come by wishing, it will only come by working it. It won't come by waiting for it, it will come by building it.

God's Word in Hebrews 3:4 says,

> **For every house is builded by some man; but he that built all things is God.**

Every glorious future requires the involvement of man

for it to be built and secure; even though in the ultimate God is the builder of all things and without Him all of man's effort equals vanity.

Partner with God to ensure the reality of that glorious future that He has in store for you. You must be ready to work in co-operation with God to make that glorious future real and not fail or suffer the risk of loss.

You cannot sit down with folded hands, waiting for or wishing a glorious future. No! Rather, now that you are still single; you must arise and co-operate with God. Work hand in hand with Him, ready to secure your glorious future. When you accept responsibility, partner with God and take the required covenant steps, you certainly secure your future.

What are these required covenant steps? Let us examine some of them here briefly.

Tame Your Thoughts.

The first covenant step towards securing your future has to do with your thought pattern. Look at the scripture in Jeremiah 29:11 again. It says:

> *For I know the thoughts that I think toward you, says the LORD, thoughts of peace and not of evil, to give you a future and a hope.*

Notice that in the above scripture, the word 'thought'

appears there twice. And then, the word 'think,' once; making it three times. So, it begins with your thinking. You know it very well that thoughts are invisible. You could seat next to someone or even sleep on the same bed together, but you never know what such a one is thinking. Someone could be seated in a place but be thousands of miles or kilometers away in his or her thoughts. Thoughts are invisible.

As invisible as your thoughts are, they are so powerful that they define your living! So, securing your future actually begins with your thought pattern. If you carry stinking thoughts, you will definitely live a stinking life. Your thoughts determine your living.

Your life is a product of your thoughts. Look at this for a moment: Whatever your course of study, if you are a student; or a career person, your actions are a product of your thoughts. Your thought pattern plays a major role in that decision. Physically, if you are standing up somewhere right now, the place you are standing is a product of your thought. If you are sitting down somewhere right now, the seat you are on is a product of your thought. May be when you came into the place where you are seated reading this material right now, there were several empty seats. You then probably had to look around, directed by your thoughts and eventually decided on the particular seat you are on right now. The clothes you have on you right now are a product of your previous thoughts. Perhaps since last night, if you select clothes in advance like me; you went through your closet and made a selection of what to wear today. Everything in your life is a product of your thoughts.

So, even though thoughts are invisible, it is the womb where your future is conceived before it can be birthed. This explains why Hebrews 11:3 says:

By faith we understand that the worlds were framed by the word of God, so that the things which are seen were not made of things which are visible. (NKJV)

To secure your future therefore, you must tame your thoughts and tailor it in the desired direction. This is crucial because your life will follow the direction of your dominant thoughts. Little wonder then that the Bible warns in Proverbs 23:7

For as he thinketh in his heart, so is he.

Clearly, your life is a product of your thoughts!

Your thoughts design your future. For example, Covenant University in Nigeria, West Africa is a reality today, but it didn't come just by wishing it. It was first conceived as a seed years before in the thoughts of someone – the chancellor, Dr. David O. Oyedepo. It is a product of thoughts. In the same vein, Faith Tabernacle, the 50-thousand seat church auditorium in Africa, built and completed within one year, debt-free is a reality today. It is acclaimed to be the largest single church auditorium in the world to date. But it was first conceived as a seed many years ago in the thoughts of the Visioner - Bishop David O. Oyedepo. Today, that property houses the international headquarters of the Living Faith Church World Outreach Center, a.k.a. Winners Chapel International.

To secure your future, you must tame your thoughts today. I can tell you this, that what you are right now is a product of your previous thoughts. Therefore, your future will be determined by your thoughts today. If you must build a glorious future, in partnership with God, it must begin with your thoughts today. The future you cannot conceive and accommodate in your thoughts today, you can never secure. Remember Genesis 13:15 says:

For all the land which thou seest, to thee will I give it, and to thy seed for ever.

To 'see' it, is to 'think' it. What kind of thoughts are you accommodating concerning your future? God is limited by your thinking. Philippians1:14 says:

But without thy mind would I do nothing; that thy benefit should not be as it were of necessity, but willingly.

In *Luke 14:28*, the Bible says:

> *For which of you, intending to build a tower, sitteth not down first, and counteth the cost, whether he have sufficient to finish it?*

Recently, I was reading this scripture, and the word 'intend' caught my attention. I then discovered that it means to have in mind, to think. Securing your future can be likened to building a tower. Just like you cannot build a tower, without first conceiving it in your thought, so you cannot secure your future, without taming your thoughts.

Your life moves in the direction of your dominant thoughts. To secure your future therefore, you must tame your thoughts. Put your thoughts under control. Sanitize your thoughts. Refuse to accommodate stinking, wild, negative nor anti-glorious thoughts! (2 Corinthians 10:3-5). Rather, focus on the positive things of life. But how do I sanitize my thoughts? You may ask. The following hints will be helpful.

Beware of what you see

There is power in pictures. The important of visual aids in teaching cannot be over-emphasized. Pictures enhance the communication process. Pictures are easy to remember. So, if your thoughts must be sanitized, you must be very selective and be careful of what you see. You will produce what you continually see!

Now that you are still single, what kind of movies do you watch? You need to gather all those un-edifying movies out of your closet and destroy them. What kind of television shows do you watch? The society at large has become so polluted by virtue of all kinds of un-edifying pictures that are all over the places. Giant billboards are now common place. Advertising agents put giant billboards that can easily corrupt the minds of people, especially the younger generation, in strategic locations.

Some magazines are filled with pictures that can easily pollute the mind. Most people who are involved in vices – homosexuality, robbery, masturbation, illicit sex, etc get enticed and entangled by what they see, especially pornographic pictures. Pornography is linked to sexual bondage.

When you surf the Internet, which websites do you visit, especially when no one is around? What you see imparts your life either positively or negatively. The private lives of some people are radically different from their public lives. You know, sin looks attractive when it tempts, but it deceives people because it poisons and destroys eventually. One day, King David looked through his window and saw Bath-she-ba, Uriah's wife and almost lost his destiny to that incidence (2 Sam. 11: 1-2). It took the grace and the mercy of God to put him back on track. The fall of Samson, an Old Testament one-man-army, began when he 'saw' a harlot and went in unto her (Judg. 16:1). He ended his journey in shame. Never give in to anything that can destroy your future. You will make it.

Many years ago, when we were living in the northern part of the country, my husband watched on video the crusade of a great man of God, Archbishop Benson Idahosa who is now gone to be with the Lord. In that video, he saw the manifestation of the power of God, healings and anointing. Innumerable healings took place. On watching it, my husband had an encounter with God. Many healings took place in the church the next Sunday service. That is the power of positive pictures.

Be mindful of what you read

I Timothy 4:13 says: *"Till I come, give attendance to reading, to exhortation, to doctrine."* But while it is important for you to develop a reading culture from your single years, you must understand that whatever you read influences your thoughts and subsequently your life, either positively or negatively. Wisdom demands that you are very selective of the materials you read. The man that eventually developed the theory of evolution, we are told was a seminarian; but he read a book that influenced him negatively and put his life in the wrong direction. Many have been taken captive and are following him today.

What do you read at your quite moments? You cannot settle down reading phonographic materials, claiming that nobody is there to see you or to rebuke you; especially because you are single and probably live alone and expect a secured future that way. In case you have any un-edifying materials such as books, magazines, etc in your possession, you must gather and destroy them immediately. Your future will not be corrupted in Jesus' name.

Be careful what you hear

Ezekiel 2:2 says: *And the spirit entered into me when he spake unto me.* The spirit of what you hear enters into you, knowingly or unknowingly. Not everything is good for your hearing. Never allow people to make you a dumping ground for junks. There are certain talks that should never be tolerated by you. Certain discussions should not be held in your vicinity. People know that no gossip is permitted in my environment. Talebearers and backbiters are never comfortable around me.

What you hear either produces faith or fear. This explains why Jesus said in Mark 4:24,

   ...Take heed what ye hear:

And in Luke 8:18,

   Take heed therefore how ye hear:

So, what you hear is as important as how you hear it. What kind of music do you listen to, especially when you are alone? What you hear often, you will surely think about and will definitely affect your future.

Watch Your Words

The second covenant step you must take to secure your future has to do with your words. Beware of what you say! Words are seeds and when you sow it, you reap it. Mark 11:23 says:

...he shall have whatsoever he saith.

Your words determine your worth. What you say determine what you have, positive or negative. In the same vein, your words determine your world. So, you can frame your world with your words. You have a duty to speak into your future to secure it. Several years ago when this ministry just began, the visioner, Bishop David Oyedepo kept declaring faith-filled words to secure the future, which has now become a reality. Back then, sometimes in a service, we could be about twenty people or less in attendance, but he kept declaring how that he could see an invisible crowd fill the auditorium with an overflow. Those were days when each worshiper could have three long benches to himself or herself, due to the attendance.

Remember what Romans 4:17 says:

..., and calleth those things which be not as though they were.

71

What you declare today determines what will be delivered to you in future. What you say sets a pace for what you see. Listen carefully, your words either spare you or snare you, the choice is yours! Speak the scripture into your future and no devil will be able to stop it from coming to pass.

Proverbs 6:2 says:

Thou art snared with the words of thy mouth, thou art taken with the words of thy mouth.

Your mouth determines your making. You will make it! This is one major principles I leant during the period when the devil attacked my body. During that time, negative thoughts always flooded by mind. I learnt to fight negative thoughts with words, then with thoughts. I learnt to watch my words, never allowing negative words come out of my mouth. Rather, I kept speaking by faith, what the scriptures have declared about my total deliverance and rescue. I kept speaking life-changing words, and slowly but surely, my circumstances began to change for the better until my total rescue was manifested.

If you learn to speak right, God can turn your pain to gain, and your pity to envy. My book titled 'Rescued From Destruction' contains the full testimony.

The experience of the Shunamite woman in II Kings 4:18-37 readily comes to mind here. In spite of the challenge she was faced with, she said: It shall be well (v. 23), It is well (v. 26). No wonder the child sneezed seven times and opened his eyes (v.35). Great lesson here - your expressions determine your experience!

So, to secure your future, it is mandatory that you watch what you say. What you say is final, no matter what the devil or people say. What do you say about your future?

Discipline Your Disposition

The third covenant step in securing your future is to discipline your disposition. Your disposition has to do with your actions, habit, usual mood and temperament. You can never secure your future without discipline. Self-discipline is the highest and best order of discipline, not the one someone else enforces on you. You must be discipline-conscious.

Do not wait for someone to run after you, before you do what is right. You have the Spirit of God inside you, so you know the right from the wrong. The Bible speaking of Jesus in Isaiah 7:15 said:

> *Butter and honey shall he eat, that he may know to refuse the evil, and choose the good.*

Your conscience is also there to give you a guide. Make self-discipline your watchword, if you desire to secure your future.

What is discipline?

Discipline means self-control. It is very important for you to be able to set boundaries for yourself for the purpose of personal discipline.

To secure your future, you must learn to discipline your disposition. You need to hear this: your disposition determines your position! Your position in future cannot be better than your disposition today.

I Samuel 2:3(b) says:

> *... for the LORD is a God of knowledge, and by him actions are weighed.*

So, God weighs your actions, dispositions, attitude, mood and positioning. Attitude greatly affects destiny. Really, your altitude in life, how high you go is determined by your attitude.

If you carry a disposition that murmurs, grumble and complain now that you are single, that already places a limit on the security of your destiny. No matter your situation, rather than murmur, give thanks and your future is guaranteed!

I know a single lady who was forty-five (45) years old and needed a breakthrough in the area of marriage. Rather than murmur and complain, she in her testimony gave thanks to God 7,000 (seven thousand times). Her miracle husband emerged and as at the time she gave her testimony, she was gloriously married. If she did not discipline her disposition, probably she would still be single till now.

I also heard of a mature single lady who needed a miracle husband. She was driving one day and had a flat tyre on the high way. She however maintained a joyful disposition, rather than being upset. While she was trying to fix it, someone whom she never knew saw her, parked by her side and assisted her get it done. He later became her miracle husband. God is still in the business of divine connections, but you must know how to discipline your disposition.

Remember Hannah in 1Samuel 1:18,

...So the woman went her way, and did eat, and her countenance was no more sad.

When she changed her disposition by removing a sad countenance, her position also changed. No matter your situation, maintain an attitude of expectancy.

Murmuring is a very terrible disposition, never give it a place so your future can be secure. Remember I Corinthians 10:10 says:

Neither murmur ye, as some of them also murmured, and were destroyed of the destroyer.

Also, in securing your future, you must be able to discipline yourself with regard to what time to sleep and what time to wake up. Discipline your taste - when to eat and what to eat. Discipline your relationships, how you handle time as well as money. Actually, your disposition in all areas of life require discipline. Set boundaries around your life. No one else can do that for you.

May your place in God's end time glorious agenda not be lost to undisciplined dispositions!

5

THE FOCUS FACTOR

The light of the body is the eye; if therefore thine eye be single, thy whole body shall be full of light.

Matthew 6:22

Focus is the key to success. That is why Satan fights hard to break your focus. If he can blur your focus, then he can mar your life. You become what you behold. Whatever you focus on consumes your time, energy, finances and attention. If you will focus on God and his kingdom whatever you are looking for will ultimately be yours.

It is important to understand the place of focus if you must be a single with a difference. It is a key factor in your quest for a life with a difference as a single. Untold distractions abound during the single years, with many issues calling for your attention. To overcome these, your eye must be single; you must be focused.

To focus means to concentrate, look ahead, and keep your attention on something. It connotes having a dream, goal or something of interest ahead of you. Therefore, it is the force or ability that propels you to forge ahead or look into the future, in order to obtain outstanding results.

One thing that stands out clearly about focus is that accepting and taking personal responsibility is absolutely necessary. No one can stay focused for you or on your behalf. It is something that you must do by yourself with God's help and enabling.

Areas of Focus

It is not everything that calls for your attention that you should focus on. When you know the necessary areas to focus on in life while single, you can safely concentrate on profiting wonderfully from them. What are these areas to focus on especially during the single years so as to live a uniquely different life? Let us examine some of them here.

God Must Have First Place

> **But seek ye first the kingdom of God, and his righteousness; and all these things shall be added unto you.**
>
> Matthew 6:33

We live in a world where so many things are vying for our attention. So, to succeed in life, one requires to focus on God by giving Him the first place. God must be your first priority and primary focus in life. When you give Him first place, you cannot be displaced in life! The place you give God in your life determines your placement in this life.

He is your ultimate source, and your goal should be to follow him wholeheartedly. He is your helper and without him there is nothing you can do. In fact without Him the purpose for your life can never be realized, because He is the determiner of purpose.

Many singles want to be married, and that is good. But much more important is to focus on God as your husband.

> *For thy Maker is thine husband; the Lord of hosts is his name; and thy Redeemer the Holy One of Israel; The God of the whole earth shall he be called.*
>
> Isaiah 54:4

You cannot have God as your husband and not be fulfilled. With Him you can not feel lonely and unloved. The first thing to do is to develop a love relationship with your Maker. Study His Word; pray (commune with him as your husband) and make up your mind to serve in His house with all diligence. At the appropriate time he will bring your way a man or woman of your dreams. What place does God occupy in your heart right now?

Your Goals, Visions And Dreams

Only goal setters are goal getters. You can only catch

goals that you are set for. A goal scorer in a football match must get himself set for goals. In like manner, a goalkeeper must stay focused on the ball if he is to catch it.

Every one who is going somewhere in life must set goals. **Goals** are things that you intend to realize and obtain. They are things that you have an objective to work towards. A **vision** is the unfolding of God's plan for an individual's life, while **dreams** are projections into the future which one looks forward to. Goals, visions and dreams give you definite expectations for the future.

For example, you can set goals to enhance your condition of living by seeking to improve your skills on your job, learning a new trade or furthering your studies. There are ways of going about this, which would not cost you much. For instance, you can read books. Even where you work, there could be someone who could teach you etc.

Knowing where you are going is as important as knowing how to get there. Focus helps you keep at your goal until you arrive at your destination. Someone wisely said, "Be a postage stamp; stick to one thing until you get there."

Isaiah 50:7 says:

For the Lord God will help me; therefore shall I not

be confounded: therefore have I set my face like a flint, and I know that I shall not be ashamed.

To focus on your goals, dreams and visions, you need to do the following:

Write your goals

As soon as you determine your goals, Satan will try to diffuse your enthusiasm by undermining them. After some time, you could forget them or even begin to wonder whether those goals would be worthwhile or not. Writing down your goals helps to keep this from happening. Don't leave them to the chance of memory. Writing your goals reinforces them in your own thinking and reminds you to stay committed to them.

Set deadlines

Setting deadlines entails putting a time frame within which you intend for the realization of your goals to take place. Someday is no day!

Develop a mental picture of your goals

Remember that Jesus always used parables to paint pictures for us to understand the word which he taught. Simply put, think about your goals. You can get things like a photograph that approximates your goal and put it where you can see it everyday. Your future is in your pictures of today. What picture do you have about your tomorrow, career, health, family, etc? Remember, until you see it, it cannot be given unto you (Genesis 13:15).

Develop a plan for reaching your goals

God never does anything without first planning for it. Planning helps you to set everything in proper perspective and appropriate order. Planning enables you to do each thing at the right time. Like in the story of creation, God did everything sequentially (Genesis1:1-31). He brought light first before any other thing in order to set the pace for all other things to be made; He brought all of man's food before making the man. Animal habitats were made even before the animals were made.

Without adequate planning, things cannot be done orderly, but rather haphazardly. It is recommended that your plans be documented also. Many people run away from planning because it seems to take more time to plan than to implement. But, at the end of the day, you will discover that it was a worthwhile exercise.

Water your goals with prayer

Goals are like plants. Without daily attention and constant care, they will shrivel up and die. What water is to plants is what prayer is to your goals. Luke 18:1. Without prayer, your goals may never see the light of day talk less of surviving.

Focus Boosters

Now that we have examined two essential areas that demand focus especially as singles, let us examine the factors that boost focus.

Develop A Superiority Complex

No matter the background you come from, if you are going to succeed in life, you must refuse to see yourself as unfortunate, because you are not. How you see and what you think about yourself determines what you will experience (Proverbs 23: 7).

You are a creature of God's deliberate purpose for glory and not shame. You are made in his image and before you ever came here He had charted a colourful destiny for you (Romans 8:28–30). Even if circumstances tell you otherwise, you are a creature of great worth in God. You are His elect and His chosen. You are a precious gem of great price. God's election and choice of you cost him the life of his only begotten son. So, change your perspective and shake yourself out of the dungeon of self-pity. You are not a misfit; you are a "proper fit" - properly fitted into divine plan.

Be Forward Looking

Focus is all about being forward looking. If you want to go forward you must keep looking forward. No one drives a car forward looking backwards. It is impossible to go forward without looking forward. Wherever you are headed is where you ought to face.

Now that you have goals, visions and dreams, those are the things you should look forward to fulfilling. You must know that while your yesterday is dead, buried and gone, today is the womb of your tomorrow. Stop bemoaning your past. No amount of reminiscing about yesterday can change it, so forget about the things that are in the past and get ready for your future by making the most of your today.

Philippians 3:13 -14 says:

> *Brethren, I count not myself to have apprehended: but this one thing I do, forgetting those things which are behind, and reaching forth unto those things which are before, I press toward the mark for the prize of the high calling of God in Christ Jesus.*

Refuse Distractions

Many things are calling for your attention. That does not make them legitimate. Youths and singles generally are known to be full of activities. When you are driving on the highway, you cannot afford to be looking every way; otherwise you will find yourself in the bush. Also, can you imagine a star athlete in a 100 meters dash looking sideways as he is running? Such an athlete can never win.

When you are not focused, you are walking in

darkness; and might stumble (Matthew 6:22). Remember Peter who almost drowned in the sea because he allowed himself to be distracted by the waves. Distractions are usually noisy; the aim is to catch your attention thereby making you look at them. When you do so, it seems you will drown under them. What distractions are you facing right now? The good news is: you can overcome them! All through scriptures, there are examples of people who remained focused despite distractions and they became uniquely different as singles.

Biblical Examples Of People Who Exhibited Focus

Joseph

As a youth, he had a dream (Genesis 37: 5). He faced, fought and overcame a lot of distractions while yet single before his dreams became a reality (Genesis 39).

Moses

In his single years, he received a mandate from the Lord to lead His people out of bondage to the Promised Land. He had to overcome distractions, God had to arrest his attention through the bush that burned with fire but was not consumed. Exodus 3:1-6

Rahab

She was a harlot in Jericho and therefore was an outcast

among her people. But she had heard that there was a God in Israel who fought for His people. Through focus, she was saved from the destruction that came upon Jericho and eventually entered the lineage of Jesus (Joshua 2 & 6).

Ruth

She was a widow and a beloved daughter-in-law to Naomi (Ruth 1-4). *D*espite every discouragement and the negative circumstances that she found herself in, she refused to be distracted. Rather, she remained focused and maintained a covenant relationship with Naomi which eventually changed her story for the better.

Widow Of Zarephath

She was the widow who fed Elijah till the end of the famine in 1 Kings 17: 8–16. Life became hard for her and her son after her husband died. Notice that in verse 9 Elijah was told that God had commanded a widow to sustain him. It therefore means that the widow had been expecting Elijah before he showed up. She had almost given up hope, but was met where she was gathering sticks with which to cook what food they had left. She had to overcome the distraction of famine, focus on the future of abundance. Therefore she promptly obeyed Elijah without any questions or arguments.

Anna, the Prophetess

As a widow, she served God with fastings and prayers

(Luke 2:36–38). She had a vision of the coming of Jesus Christ and saw it fulfilled. When you catch a vision or have goals and dreams that are divine, nothing can kill you before your time!

Apostle Paul

Formerly known as Saul, he persecuted the Church of Jesus Christ. There was a divine mandate on his life. To arrest his attention, there had to shine round about him a light from heaven. *Acts 9: 1- 22*. He later became an apostle. And the list goes on and on. You also have to fight distractions, maintain focus, so you can be distinguished and fulfill destiny.

Focus Breakers

Focus, I have said, is giving your undivided attention to something. What the devil tries to do is to break your focus by bringing all kinds of obstacles to distract you, because he knows that so much power can be wielded through focus. We therefore need to be able to recognize these obstacles. What are these focus breakers? These are some of them:

Self-Condemnation

Self-condemnation and sin consciousness make you take your eyes off God and your goals by capitalizing on your past. Self condemnation says things such as

"You don't deserve anything good from God, because of your filthy past. Even people who are more righteous than you have not made a headway in life yet, and you think that God will bypass them to bless you? No way!"

The enemy wants to make you believe that God is against you. The good news is that God does not judge you by your past if you are born again (Hebrews 10:17). At new birth, you become a new creature and all old things became history; your life and all things about you becomes new,

> **Therefore if any man be in Christ, he is a new creature: old things are passed away; behold, all things are become new.**
>
> 2 Corinthians 5: 17

Refuse to walk in self-condemnation because God does not condemn you.

Feelings Of Insecurity And Instability

These feelings are the results of double mindedness, and a double-minded person cannot attain to anything in life (James. 1:8). Knowledge will solve the problem of insecurity and instability.

God is your security; and knowledge of his provision for your future will stabilize your life.

> **The LORD will destroy the house of the proud: but**

he will establish the border of the widow

Proverbs 15: 25

'Widow' in this passage does not only mean a woman who has lost her husband, but could also mean "the desolate." To be referred to as desolate means one who is deserted; devoid of hope, comfort, warmth; one that is abandoned, neglected, forsaken, deprived, alone, sad wretched etc. In case you have used any of these adjectives to describe yourself in time past, whether in your thoughts or words; you can see from the above scripture that God is very mindful of you! And as believers, we walk by faith, not by feelings! (2 Corinthians 5:7).

Inferiority Complex

Inferiority Complex gets you preoccupied with your inadequacies and shortcomings. *Never see yourself as an ordinary insignificant single somewhere on earth who do not deserve any kind of attention from God. You must understand that* you are so precious and of a great price to God – you cost Him the precious blood of Jesus and He even knows your name (1 Peter 1:19; 2:9; Isaiah 43:4).

Offences

Offences are an expression of inward anger and animosity. It could be either or both towards God and man. Offences cut you off from focusing on God for the fulfillment of your destiny to focusing on what you think he has been done against you. You must settle it in your heart that God is not the author of any misfortune that you might have faced or are facing right now in life.

Have you just lost your job? Have you just gone through a broken relationship and someone has just jilted you, having waited for a spouse for so long? Have you just lost a loved one? Do you think you do not look as naturally beautiful as you would have wanted? Do you think your body frame is not to your advantage? No matter your situation, refuse to be offended in God. If you are offended in God, then who will help you? The devil is the culprit who hitherto hid behind your ignorance. Now that you have caught him, don't allow him to escape.

Many people may have ridiculed and mocked you because of your present situation or predicament, but it is only a distraction to break your focus from your destination. Offences result in bitterness, which corrupts destinies (Hebrews 12:15).

Remember John the Baptist. Through offences, his life was cut short, thereby terminating his most enviable and glorious destiny, (Matthew 11: 6).

Beware of offences. They harden the heart and blind you

to God's goodness. Therefore, from your heart, let go anyone towards whom you have offences (Matthew 18:34, 35).

Fear

Fear is the loss of courage in the face of awareness of danger. It is the expectation of evil etc. Fear is faith in the devil's whisperings and reports. Fear of what? Fear of the unknown, the present, the future or even of the past. Fear paralyses initiative, focus and activity. Fear disallows its victims from planning.

Be aware that fear is a spirit, and that is not the kind of spirit that God has given to you. He has not given us the spirit of fear, but of power (courage, boldness), love and a sound mind (2 Timothy 1:7).

Wrong Association

The people you associate with can either make or mar your focus in life and destiny. 1 Corinthians 15:33 implies from its contents that *good association builds and enhances your focus, thereby making a better person out of you. Never associate with or be a friend to someone who lacks focus; else you will soon lose focus yourself.* Therefore weigh your relationships; separate yourself from anybody that focuses neither on God nor any divine goal.

Remember,

He that walketh with wise men shall be wise: but a

companion of fools shall be destroyed.

Proverbs 13: 20

Whoever wants to be your friend must acknowledge and recognize the God you are serving. The person must also respect your goals, visions and dreams. This means that anyone who mocks or discourages you from serving God or realizing your goals is an enemy and must never be allowed to be your friend.

Rewards Of Focus

The power that focus wields manifests in rewards/ benefits and is able to affect every area of your life. Some of them include the following.

Speed

When you are focused and you know where you are going in life, you gain speed. Your life is full of light when you are focused, so you can see properly. This facilitates your speed (Matthew 6: 22). When you know where you are going, you are able to arrive there in good time. The clearer you see, the faster you can move.

Stress-Free Accomplishments

Know this, that on your path to the fulfillment of your goals are the provisions - spiritual, mental, financial, and physical -, which you need to arrive there. There is minimal stress on the way to achieving your goals. God is faithful who has inspired the goals, visions and dreams in you, and He will also ensure their accomplishment (1 Thessalonians 5:24).

Success

Focus helps you to attain your goals and a goal attained is success obtained. The more you look ahead and above, the farther and higher you go. The more of God you focus on the more like Him you become. Remember you become like unto whatever you adore (2 Corinthians 3:18).

Peace and Joy

When you focus on God, peace and joy attend to your steps, your life, your family, your children etc. (Hebrews 12:2). Focus infuses much joy such that mundane things around you do not move you any more.

Restorations

Restoration means a returning to store. What is to be returned to store? Everything the enemy has stolen! When God secured the attention of the children of Israel, restoration was the result (Joel 2:25–27). God will restore to you all the years and goods that the devil has stolen from you.

So much has been said, now the ball is firmly in your court. Stay focused and become a single with a difference in this end time. May that be your testimony in Jesus' name!

Chapter 6

SINGLE AND USEFUL

Remember now thy Creator in the days of thy youth,
while the evil days come not, nor the years draw nigh,
when thou shalt say, I have no pleasure in them;

Ecclesiastes 12:1

As a single, you are created to be useful. The single years are the prime time of life when all you see ahead and all that bubbles within you is life. It is a very precious gift you hold in your hands, which others wish they could recall. God gave you this gift, so you can fully utilize it. Single days ought to be useful days! Now that you are still single, how useful are you?

God has put in you certain unique deposits to enhance your usefulness while single. These include but are not limited to the following.

Unusual strength

Young people are synonymous with strength. The scripture acknowledges this strength in 1 John 2:14

that says:

> *...I have written unto you, young men, because ye*
> *are strong, and the word of God abideth in you, and*
> *ye have overcome the wicked one.*

God expects you to channel this unusual strength positively and correctly. The physical strength that a twenty-five (25) year old would exert, a fifty (50) year old, may not be able to. Your physical energy is at its best in the days of your youth, while you are still single. With this unusual strength, pursuit of your vision is easy and you will be most useful.

Passion/Zeal

While single, you can demonstrate tireless diligence and an enthusiastic devotion to a cause. The passion to serve, the zeal to run is there in you and is usually very high (Ecclesistes 12:1). There are many examples of singles in the Bible who made use of the zeal they had for God to accomplish great things.

David's passion for God helped him to kill Goliath. Joshua from his youth had been going to war; so, he was not afraid to declare good report about the promised land. Joseph as a youth was a good ambassador in Egypt, despite his pitiable condition. This passion or zeal is there in you also and can be utilized in the pursuit of your God-given purpose in life; so, make full use of it.

Great and innovative ideas

And it shall come to pass afterward, that I will pour out my spirit upon all flesh; and... your young men shall see visions"

Joel 2:28

We are in the days of great inventions and innovations among youths and singles. This is because the mind is still young and void of unnecessary worries, concerns and anxiety. As a Godly single that possesses the mind of Christ (1 Corinthians 2:16), you can think and add values in diverse areas or disciplines of life. Daniel and the three Hebrew boys were able to get answers to the challenge on ground via insightful knowledge of God.

Your worth and value in life, determines your usefulness. By seeing yourself the way God sees you, you will be able to add colour to your world and generation at large. The importance of the subject of the usefulness of a single cannot be over-emphasized.

However, let us look at different ways in which singles can be useful.

At Home

From whom the whole body fitly joined together and compacted by that which every joint supplieth, according to the effectual working in the measure of every part, maketh increase of the body unto the edifying of itself in love.

Ephesians 4:16

God, who is a God of purpose, intentionally brought you to this world through your particular family. You did not just come into existence. He brought you into the world through your family so you can be a useful contributor and to make a positive impact on the well being of that home.

All the parts of the physical body are joined together and perform specific functions: so also you are brought into the world through your home to play a definite essential role. You have to play your part to enhance the success of that home; so work at it. You are a joint in that family network and there is a measure of success to be supplied by you for the edifying of it. Be a useful joint!

Acts 1:8 says:

But ye shall receive power, after that the Holy Ghost is come upon you: and ye shall be witnesses unto me both in Jerusalem, and in all Judea, and in Samaria, and unto the uttermost part of the earth.

Charity, it is said, begins from home. It does not end there, but it begins from there. Your home or family is your Jerusalem and your usefulness, as a single should begin from there. Until you are useful at home, there is no guarantee that you will be useful outside the home.

How best can you be effective at home now that you are still single?

By serving your parents in love

Be involved in household chores; see every opportunity to serve at home as service unto the Lord and not just to your parents or family members. Learn to and be practically involved in house cleaning, cooking, laundry, mowing, etc. By so doing, you magnetize parental blessings and their heart blesses you. Many youths and singles lack these skills today; many cannot even cook simple meals and this is affecting them a great deal, even in their relationships.

Remember, whatever skills you acquire stay with you all your lifetime and become yours. So, stop shifting responsibilities to others! Stop waiting for other family members to do what you ought to do at home. The interesting thing is, as you get involved in household chores, you get used to them, thereby perfecting your skills in such areas. Such skills later become assets to you in the future.

Before I got married, all the detailed household chores I learnt and was involved in are now beneficial to me, even though back then it was not convenient. Even if

your parents are difficult to please and complain, never
be discouraged nor give up; rather, serve from your heart
as unto the Lord.

As a matter of fact, you will be sowing a very good
seed into your own future and your harvest is sure. In
fact, there is a sparing for a son that serves and a
marking out between him that serves and him that
doesn't (Malachi 3: 17-18).

In the Church

David as a young man delighted in the things of
God and this is one of his secrets. He said,

> *I was glad when they said unto me, Let us go into*
> *the house of the Lord*
>
> Psalms 122:1

The house of God, your local church, should be your
second home. Just as you will naturally discharge your
responsibilities at home, so also you should not be
compelled to serve in the house of God. You can locate
an area where your strength can be channeled and rightly
utilized in the church. For example, if you have a good
voice, the choir might be a good place for you to serve.
Or, if you cannot sing, you can sweep, join those who
are involved in cleaning. You do not need any special
talent to keep the house of God clean. You can be
involved in the area of evangelism.

Many opportunities abound. You only need to prayerfully make a choice that will enhance your destiny. Refuse to be a bench warmer in church, who only attend services. It is when you serve that you expect to be blessed but never gets involved in, nor contributes in any way to what goes on there (Ephesians 4: 16).

Invest your single days to serve the Lord wholeheartedly. Make impact in the church; edify the body of Christ. Do it with the integrity of your heart. Do not allow anything to distract you. This time is a great opportunity for you; so, serve God unreservedly with unbroken focus, undisturbed by family responsibilities.

Find a need and fill it! Quality service unto God prevents aimless wondering. Ever since I gave my life to Christ as a teenager, I have always been involved in active service in the kingdom of God at one level or another. It was the same with my husband before we got married. All our children are involved in kingdom service at different levels also.

I had served in the prayer squad, choir, as a counselor to new converts, as one of those cleaning the church, house fellowship coordinator, praise leader, etc. It will interest you to note that I still compose sing-able songs up till now, even though I no longer serve in the choir!

Matthew 6: 33 says:

Seek ye first the kingdom of God, and his righteousness; and all these things shall be added unto you.

When you make God first, even in service, He also makes you a first class citizen of the earth. Make kingdom service your priority and you will enjoy all other things that life and salvation have to offer as additions. If your purpose for living does not include serving the Lord, then you do not have a right purpose for living. Whatever you do now is an investment, so put in your best in the church.

Let your Pastor give thanks to God for the gift of your person. Most of the giants of faith today knew God in their youth, stayed with Him in service and today by this light that they encountered in their single days, they are positively imparting millions on earth through their message and outreach materials. You too can do the same.

In the Society

You need to make positive contributions in your society, beginning with the community where you live. In scriptures, many imparted their communities, societies and nations while yet single. Here are some of them, and you can do the same thing and even much more.

David

He solved a national problem by saving the whole nation from shame; he refused failure. With his rich knowledge of the God of Israel and the abundance of testimony that he had, he took off Goliath's head and the glory and victory was given to the God of Israel (ISamuel 17: 3-55). That special testimony of yours can be an eye opener for others in your community that will let them know that your God is alive.

Joseph

He utilized his special gift of the interpretations of dreams to preserve the nation where he sojourned. He was used in averting famine that would have consumed even his people (Genesis 41). He gave ideas that brought about economic empowerment for the nation of Egypt. That gift in you, that special skill may be what your society will need for a time like this.

Nehemiah

He was a nation builder (Nehemiah 2: 5). He took the courage to raise and rebuild the ruined city wall of Jerusalem.

Esther

A fearless lady that saw herself as an ambassador of her people in the king's court, she preferred to die than to see her people destroyed unjustly (Esther 4).

All these people among several others were useful singles that imparted or added value to their society. You are the next on the line!

Even if you are a student, in your school or college, seek to be a contributor, to your colleagues, teachers and lecturers, even the school authorities. Refuse to be identified with hooliganism, but for positive impact.

My husband, Dr. David O. Oyedepo often tells a story of how he was deployed to work as a teacher in a little settlement down the western part of Nigeria many years ago. On arrival, he noticed that there was no single church in that village. He said to himself that he would not leave that village without planting a church. He was not a pastor as at that time neither was he sent there as a missionary.

Through his determination and by the special grace of God, he successfully planted a vibrant church in the place and on his send forth day, he was presented with a local bush lantern. The head of that community acknowledged the spiritual light, the gospel of Jesus that he brought to their land and he prayed that this light of God in him would shine round the whole world. Today, proofs abound of that great light he brought into the lives of many.

You can do likewise and much better. Give Him your

best and He will make you the best.

Covenant Responsibilities

God is a God of covenants. He believes in, respects and does not break covenants. When man keeps his own side of the covenant, God keeps His as well (Psalms 89:34).

Life, as you know is all about responsibilities. To be useful, you must be responsible! For you to be useful in the areas discussed above, you need to understand and accept your covenant responsibilities. These cut across the three areas of man's being – spirit, soul and body (1 Thessalonians 5: 23). Let us now examine each of these briefly here.

Spiritually

You cannot be useful at home, church and society outside of God (John 15:5). Your usefulness and relevance starts with God, the Author and Finisher of your faith. Your level of spirituality is the foundation that determines the level of your usefulness in life.

The Bible says in Romans 8: 6

> *To be carnally minded is death; but to be spiritually minded is life and peace.*

You must accept responsibility spiritually, for you to be useful. For anything to work in your life, your walk with God must first be in place. To enhance your walk with God and spiritual responsibility, you must pay a close attention to these areas.

Study God's Word Regularly

Be committed to the study of God's word now that you are still single. God's word is the manual for living, go for it. Read your Bible! Become a word addict. Bend down and study the word, daily (2 Timothy 2:15). Personally, until I have spent time in the word, the day is not properly set and I tell my biological children the same thing. I tell you, it works!

Make a decision, commitment and covenant that no day will pass you by as a single, without spending adequate time in the word. Never be ashamed of the gospel or being found with a Bible in your hand (Luke 9:26).

Never get too busy for the word. Read it, study it, chew it, meditate on it and then put it to work! Thereafter, without any doubt, your profiting will appear to all in the level of your usefulness all around you.

Spend Quality Time in Prayer

Set time aside for qualitative time in prayer, now that you are still single. Even Jesus, the Son of God made time to pray. Only those who know how to kneel before God in prayer, ever stand tall before men and circumstances in life. Just like you spend time to talk and commune with your biological father, friends, colleagues and peers, in the same vein you should spend time communing with God, your heavenly father in prayer.

Researchers have proved that we spend 70% of our waking time communicating and we spend 30% of it talking. It is crucial and wise to learn to commune much more with God. The more you commune with God in prayer, the more you radiate His glory, command more exploits and the more useful you become in life.

God is the source of your being. Pray and commune with Him in your understanding and in tongues. It is not necessarily how long you pray, but it is how well and the heart from where it is coming that matter. There is a rich deposit of God's grace in you, stir it up in prayer and it will be manifest for others to see.

Fellowship Constantly

Never become too busy that you cannot find time to attend fellowship with other believers (Hebrews 10:25). The effectiveness and beauty of a broom is when it is in a bunch. So also, your effectiveness, beauty and relevance will be more outstanding when you fellowship regularly.

Remember, Psalms 84:7 says:

They go from strength to strength, every one of them
in Zion appeareth before God.

Be addicted to fellowship. Go to church regularly. Learn to be in the right place at the right time. I have come to understand that when you go to church, you do not only have fellowship with God, but also with angels, the spirit of just men made perfect and with one another! Oh, what a unique time!

For me, church time is usually an exciting one. I eagerly look forward to it, because among other things it brings refreshing for me. It is the same thing for all my family members. Get excited and rejoice in church, it is your father's house! Whatever wants to drive you away from church, wants to drive you away from your father's house, Don't let it!

Mentally

To be useful, relevant and valuable in life, you must be mentally alert.

Isaiah 1:18 says:

Come now, and let us reason together, saith the
LORD...

To reason means to have sound judgments. Your mind has to operate at heaven's frequency. Your level of reasoning determines your level of rising in life. You cannot rise, stand out, be useful and contributive without being mentally sound.

You must have sound judgments and be realistic in your approach to life. Never build your life on assumptions or fantasy. My husband usually says assumption is the mother of frustration. To leave your life to assumption is to end up in destruction. You shall not be destroyed.

So, be practical and real, not hypocritical. Stop daydreaming. For example, if you are into a relationship that is not working and each time you remember it fear grips you, sound judgment lets you know you need to quit as fast as possible.

Be sensible and sensitive. Make a covenant with God for purity. You can be morally pure in this impure world. Keep yourself pure (1 Timothy 4: 12). Do not involve yourself in pre-marital sex; it is more dangerous than cancer! It is the New Testament forbidden fruit; flee it! Keep your sexual appetite under control. Your sex drive must be in neutral until you are covenantly married.

Set boundaries! Your memory will not be as kind to you as God, so be careful! Remember that you cannot hide from your own flesh; it will amount to attempting to hide behind one finger, which is foolishness. Even when you are in a relationship, sexual sanity must be maintained.

By the special grace of God, not by my own righteousness, I can boldly declare that my husband is the only man I have ever known all my life! Your own testimony can even be stronger.

Learn to ask relevant questions when necessary. Only those who ask questions, qualify for answers. Ask those who have correct answers. You can also go for counseling when necessary. However, this must be sought from godly people who have proofs. No matter your level, there will always be those who know more and are ahead of you; all you need is wisdom to locate them.

Also, you have to constantly sharpen your mind and update your knowledge by reading educative materials. Read materials that have to do with what you want to do or what you are involved in. This will help you to be current and enhance your level of relevance and usefulness in life. For instance, it you are involved in or want to go into buying and selling, get educative materials, books and magazines on marketing strategies from godly proven authors. Remember that readers are leaders.

In addition, further your education as much as possible. You must understand that to earn more, you have to learn more. When you learn more, it enhances your dignity and self esteem. Further your education.

Reach out for new horizons. There is no end to learning. Update yourself, develop and refuse stagnation. Enlarge your knowledge base; this will in turn enhance your level of usefulness.

Finally, think more than you talk! Until you think covenant thoughts, your life will stink (Proverbs 23:7). Many young people spend a lot of time talking, chatting, whiling away time in the name of hanging out with friends. While this in itself is not wrong, it must be controlled (Phillipians vs 14). You cannot make a difference until you know how to think more than you talk. And of course, fellowship with people of like mind (Proverbs 27:17). The kind of people you fellowship with determine your usefulness in life.

Physically

To be useful as a single, you must accept responsibility physically.

Proverbs 22:29 says

Seest thou a man diligent in his business? He shall stand before kings; he shall not stand before mean men.

Diligence is a requirement in the school of exploits; embrace it at all cost. Shun idleness. Fight laziness. Flee indolence. Embrace diligence. Be hard working. Remember that hard work never kills. In actual fact, laziness and slothfulness are what destroy, not hard work (Ecclesistes 10: 18).

Possess Working Hands

In order for you to be a single that is useful, you must possess working hands. Find something doing because God is only committed to prosper the works of your hand. If you are doing nothing, there is no channel through which God can bless and reward you. Let your hands be working hands in order for you to be a blessing to others. Do not keep waiting for a particular job. Whatever your hands find to do while looking for what you want, as long as it is not sinful or anti-covenant, begin to do it with all your might and what you are looking for, will meet you in the process.

Proverbs 10:4 says:

He becometh poor that dealeth with a slack hand: but the hand of the diligent maketh rich.

Idleness is an enemy of destiny; do not give it room. God hates idleness and laziness, so fight it! There are many young people today who are so lazy. They love pleasure and fashion. All they are waiting for is cheap and quick money. Young people commit most crimes. Stop waiting for what people will give things to you. While this in itself is not wrong, it is better if you are the one to give things to others that the other way round.

Obviously, what you don't work for never enhances

your worth. In Matthew 20:1-7, Jesus met some people at different hours of the day and He told them to go into the vineyard because there was always something for everybody to do. Work is what enhances your worth. In fact, it is so important that I Thessalonians 3:10 even says, that you should not eat if you would not work!

Acquire Necessary Skills

The importance of skill acquisition cannot be over-emphasized if you must be useful, especially as a single. Skills acquired and developed will make you an expert. Only experts excel and expertise is a product of exercise.

2 Chronicles 2: 8 says:

> **Send me also cedar trees, fir trees, and algum trees, out of Lebanon: for I know that thy servants can skill to cut timber in Lebanon; and, behold, my servants shall be with thy servants,**

This was a period of preparation for the building of the temple and only the services of skillful men were needed.

Skill is acquired and developed through practice. God gives special talents to people but there is need for these talents to be properly schooled. If you are not skilled in a job or venture, no matter how hard you pray, you will not experience breakthroughs. Skill helps you to remain relevant in your area of discipline.

Skill is not just a function of the certificate you carry or qualification you possess; it is much more of the expertise and strategies you can apply in handling your assignment. In the market place, papers have no value; it is products that sell.

You can acquire skill by going for special courses in your field or by staying on a job through patience (Romans 5:4). Do not pant after the salary that is paid; rather seek to acquire more skill. You can also acquire skill by apprenticeship (Hebrews 6:12), by exercising your efforts towards achieving your dream (James. 2: 17) and through sincere self-appraisal.

When you put all these to work, you will definitely stand out among your equals; distinguished as a single with a difference, impacting and affecting your world positively. The topmost top in life is waiting for you as a single, as you accept your covenant responsibility to get there. Even the sky is not your limit!

7

CHARACTER IS CRUCIAL!

*For yourselves know how ye ought to follow us: for
we behaved not ourselves disorderly among you;*

2 Thessalonians 3:7

One of the crucial areas of life that require serious attention, if you must live a unique and different life as a single, is your character. I must tell you this: there is no better time to build a strong Christian character than during your single years. Without any doubt, character is crucial!

Simply defined, character is someone's way of behaviour; it is a pattern of behaviour that shows moral strength, self-discipline and of course, dignity. It is your life style. It is the quality that forms the pattern of an individual's behavior. Another version of the scripture just quoted above says, "...*For we behave not ourselves irresponsively among you.*"

I can tell you with every sense of responsibility that you cannot amount to much in life, without good character. It is the platform for sustainable exploits and a glorious future. No matter your charisma, if you lack character, you will crash! Many glorious destinies have crashed for lack of character. Truly, good character is the only way out of a life of crises!

Believers were first called Christians at Antioch because they lived, behaved and demonstrated the attributes of Christ in their day-to-day living: in actions, words and deeds.

> *And the disciples were called Christians first in Antioch.*
>
> Acts 11:26(b)

Character is a seed that guarantees good and enviable harvest in later years. It is the only way to make the most of your single years. Interestingly, character is not a gift; it has to be consciously cultivated. You don't wait for it and you certainly cannot wish for it. For everyone who desires to live a godly life it is important to consciously and deliberately cultivate godly character.

In this chapter, I will be sharing with you some gems to help you cultivate, develop, grow, sustain and become a man or a woman of good Christian character. Is this really possible? You may ask. Yes, it is possible! I know it is, because it is working in my own life, in the lives of my children and family members, as well as in the lives of many other Christians that I know. However, God's word makes it very clear that to whom much is given, much is expected. You will not be a disappointment to destiny!

Without a doubt, God has a great and colourful future for everyone that is His child, including you! However, it is one thing for God to have a plan for us, but it is an entirely different thing for us to walk in that plan. It is with godly character that we can lay a solid foundation for that colourful future that God has in store for us.

Now, there are certain fundamental truths about character that you need to understand, especially now that you are still single. A good understanding of them, when appropriated will enhance your usefulness in your life journey. Let's examine some of them here:

Fundamental Truths About Character

It's a Matter of the Heart: As a seed, character has its root, base, foundation in the heart; the inner man. It doesn't end there, but it starts there. So, it is essentially a matter of the inside, which eventually finds expression on the outward. In other words, it begins from within. Proverbs 23:7 tell us,

> *For as he thinketh in his heart, so is he: Eat and drink, saith he to thee; but his heart is not with thee.*

Therefore, character begins in the heart, but it does

not stop there, it flows out. Character cannot be hidden! No matter how hard you try; sooner or later the true stuff of which you are made, will come to the open. You cannot be separated from your character. Whatever you are doing now is an overflow of what goes on inside. That is why Jesus said that if you cleanse the inside of a cup, the outside would also be clean (Matthew 23:26).

So then, to develop a godly character requires you working on your inner man first and foremost.

It is Your True Beauty: Really, your true beauty is not just in the outfit, fashionable shoes, jewelry, powder or make-up that you wear; but much more in your character.

I have observed that youths and singles generally have a high taste for fashion, beauty and excellent packaging; they pay a lot of attention to their outward man. They know the entire different, latest and current designer outfits and would go for them irrespective of the cost. To the elderly, this may not mean much.

What about perfumes, sunshades and the rest of it? They have all kinds of names, you know the different makes and you have them tucked in your wardrobes. All these are not out of place in themselves, but may I tell you something, your true clothing, your true beauty, your true smell is your character. If you wear the latest designer clothes, shoes, jewelry, perfume etc, but without character, you have no true beauty and therefore have no future!

Let's face it; to lack character is to be naked! To lack character is to stink; to lack character is to be ugly. Character is your true beauty! Thank God for all the new kinds of body lotions and the entire cosmetic collections that are now available; all of these have their place but none of them can equal nor take the place of a good character. Your true clothing; your true beauty and your true smell is your character.

It is Not a Gift: The third fact about character that you must understand is that it is not a gift. Never say such a thing as: "Well, God understands that I don't have the gift of character; or the way I am, is a function of how I was brought up by my parents!" Well, thank God for your background. Whether you were brought up by godly parents or not, you have to now accept responsibility over your life. You have no one to blame! As a believer, you are now a chosen generation, a royal priesthood, a holy nation, a peculiar people; you are now in a new place in God. It is a life of a new order.

Character, good behavior is something that those who require it cultivate consciously. In other words, if you desire good behavior, you don't wait for it, you cultivate it. That is why you will need to pay great attention to how to cultivate character, so that your nakedness can be covered and your destiny can be secured. However, before we examine the 'how' of character, let us consider the 'why' of it first.

The Why Of Character

You need to understand why good character is so crucial and important to profitable living. If you do, you will not take it lightly; rather, you will be willing to pay the price required to cultivate, develop, nurture and sustain it. Please be aware that when you exhibit good character, you are the one to benefit: it is for your good, profiting, blessing, advancement and promotion.

It Is The Foundation Of Your Future

No matter how beautiful a building looks on the outside, if there is a fault in the foundation, give it some time and it will collapse like a pack of cards. The strength and the future of any physical building lie in its foundation. To have a crack at the foundation of any building is for the security of that building to be out of place.

What a physical foundation is to a building is what character is to your destiny. So, your future has a lot to do with your character. When character is lacking in the life of anyone, that individual has no future. A life that lacks character can be likened to a building with a faulty foundation and a collapse is inevitable! Your character is the foundation of your future. In the book of Psalms 11:3, the Bible tells us,

> *If the foundations be destroyed what can the righteous do?*

Sadly, for many young people today, the subject of character is not a priority. Many do not approach the subject with any sense of seriousness. The philosophy of some young people today is: Everybody else is doing it, so why not me? Remember, you are not 'everybody'; that everybody is doing it does not make it right. Your world is waiting for you; you cannot afford to waste away! You are created to effect necessary changes, not just in your nation, but also in your generation. Please, arise to your responsibility and build your character.

> *For David, after he had served his own generation by the will of God, fell on sleep, and was laid unto his fathers, and saw corruption:*
>
> Acts 13:36

David served his own generation; it is now your turn to ensure you lay a solid foundation of character, so you also can serve your own generation. You will not disappoint your generation in Jesus name.

Why else do I need to cultivate Godly character?

It Is The Stabilizer Of Your Destiny

In some countries, stabilizers, which are used to control the flow of electricity, are very common. They simply help to regulate electrical current and ensure that all your electrical gadgets are secure and free from sudden damage. You can be sure of safety because your stabilizer is in place.

In the same way, the future of anyone that lacks character can be neither stable nor secure. You must have heard about people dying from electrical shock, that is how that destiny is bound to go through a shock when character is lacking. That shock may eventually lead to death.

Your future is too colourful; you cannot afford to joke with it! Your destiny is too precious, you cannot toy with it; your future is too glorious you will not go through 'destiny shock!'

For lack of good character, many young people lose their jobs, injure their health, destroy good relationships and mess up their destinies. Therefore, connect your life to the destiny stabilizer, which is character and you will get to your glorious destiny in God in Jesus name.

Another reason why you need to cultivate godly character is:

To Avoid Being A Hypocrite

Many people live like chameleons. When they are in a place where eyes are on them, they behave in a particular way, but when they get to where they know that they are not being watched, they behave differently. They live a life of double standards. You can never be sure of how they will behave, given certain conditions, they are unstable as water. This kind of life holds no future for anyone. You must understand that your actions will eventually catch up with you.

If you are a student for instance, allow God's Word to go through you, change and transform you. Don't be one thing at home and then be something else on campus. Stop pretending to be who you are not! After all, who are you deceiving? One of my favourite character moulding scriptures is Proverbs 15: 3, which says:

The eyes of the Lord are in every place, beholding the evil and the good.

So, no matter where you are, whether in your hostel, in the classroom, at home during holiday time, in your place of primary assignment, on your job, alone by yourself or in the midst of people, *the eyes of the Lord are in every place beholding the evil and the good.* No matter where you are per time, God's eyes are there. Do not join the company of those who live hypocritical lives. When you cultivate Godly character, you are the same in the night; the same at daytime; the same on campus; the same at home. Wherever you find yourself, you are constant and that way God's hand comes upon you for good. You will make it because God is on your side!

Attributes Of A Godly Character

If character is this important, then what are some of the attributes that make it up? It is very important for us to understand this, so you know when and where it exists and how to measure up. Let's consider some of them here.

Honesty

Providing for honest things, not only in the sight of the Lord, but also in the sight of men.

2 Corinthians 8:21

Honesty is a state of truthfulness and you know truth is power! Sometime ago, my husband, the Chancellor of Covenant University, a few of our senior pastors and myself were privileged to visit a great man of God. This man of God, who is about 106 years old and still going strong, uses no walking stick. He is still thinking and talking soundly. He is full of energy and power and still preaches powerful messages. This man is a sign and a wonder to his generation. When he was speaking he said, "You know the secret of my longevity? Truth, truth and truth."

Nothing empowers people like truth! When they were looking for people to make leaders in *Acts 6*, the Bible says they looked for honest men. Your throne in life is waiting for you, but it takes honesty for you to ascend it. Your throne another one will not take!

How do I know an honest man? An honest man tells the truth, he is straightforward, and he does not cheat. Dishonesty is the opposite of honesty and it destroys. When you are found dishonest, one of the things that happen is that you lose respect with people and as kings and priests on the earth, respect should be a part of your life. But the only way for you to enjoy respect is to be honest.

Let your yea be yea and let your nay be nay. If you call something white today, don't call the same thing black tomorrow. That will be dishonesty. Dishonesty always traps and catches up with its victims. For you not to be trapped by dishonesty, you need to make a decision for honesty today!

Take for instance, someone who cheats in an examination hall, he is simply saying by his/her actions that he or she has no regards for character building. You may be thinking that if what you are doing doesn't hurt anybody else, it's okay! Whether it is examination malpractice, immorality or any other act of dishonesty, as long as it is a sin, it is not okay. Certainly, not with

God and definitely not with your destiny! Why? Because your actions have a way of affecting not just you, but other people around you. Your actions have a way of affecting your character. You need to take this very seriously; dishonesty should never be associated with you anymore!

Discipline

This is another major attribute and component of character. Discipline is self-control; it is the willingness to take orders. It affects all aspects of your life, from punctuality to your attitude and of course to accountability. As priests and kings, if you must ascend your throne, you must be disciplined. Talking about order, the Bible says:

> **Let all things be done decently and in order.**
>
> 1 Corinthians14: 40

Therefore taking to order is discipline. For instance, at many of our higher institutions, there are rules and regulations that govern the operations. A disciplined student will comply with the rules and regulations of his or her institution.

To be disciplined is to have self-control. Chances are if you cannot control your life, then you can never be in control in life. It is important for you therefore to put control valves around your life. Embrace orderliness and self-control. Create laws for yourself and live by them. The Bible tells us in 1 Corinthians 6: 12,

> *All things are lawful unto me, but all things are not expedient: all things are lawful for me, but I will not be brought under the power of any.*

As one who is disciplined, you will choose what is expedient above what is lawful, so that your life can be under the control of God's Word.

The question then is: What are the areas of life where discipline is required?

Take for example in the area of **time**. You must be time disciplined. There is a popular saying: punctuality is the soul of business. Handle your time with every sense of discipline. If you have no respect for time, with time you will surely lose respect in life. As a student, be punctual to class; as a worker, arrive your office right on time; be in the right place at the right time. Don't allow yourself to be labelled as a 'latecomer'. It shows lack of discipline.

Think about this for a moment: if you waste 10 minutes every day, at the end of one week, you have wasted 70 minutes. At the end of a year that has accumulated to 3,650 minutes which is far above 60 hours- just in one year! May the Lord give you understanding.

Time is life. To waste time is to waste life. Don't be the kind of person that always goes late for every function. Discipline yourself in the use of time. Time can neither be stopped nor stored; it ought to be invested. From this day forward you shall be time disciplined!

Another area of discipline for instance is with money. Oh I know one thing that youths and singles everywhere like to do a lot, is to spend money. They know how to spend it. It doesn't take them time. I will like to remind everyone of you as youths, your parents have worked so hard and are still working so hard to put you through school, so don't be a waster of money and resources.

You are daily at every hamburger shop, Coca Cola stand; you take groundnut on the left hand and popcorn on the right and you have some malt drink in your handbag.

Be disciplined in your handling of money so you don't mourn in life! Be accountable, first and foremost to God and then to your parents, guardians, sponsors as well as yourself.

If you cannot handle money well now while you are still single, chances are that it will be much more difficult for you, latter in life when responsibilities start calling for your attention. For many youths and singles, money controls them, rather than they control it. They are happier when money is available. They murmur, complain, and get sad when they are broke. Never let money control your life.

Another area where you need discipline is in your sleep. There is time for everything, including sleep. As a student, you don't go to your lecture halls and begin to dose in class. It is a sign of indiscipline.

Many years ago, my husband did an exposition that has stayed with me over the years. He said if you sleep eight hours every day out of the 24 hours, then you are sleeping one third of your lifetime. So, if you live for instance to be 120 years old and you sleep eight hours of every day, you have spent how many years sleeping? 40 good years of solid sleep! Wow! Incredible!

While sleep is a requirement for living, you have to be disciplined to handle it well. You are not here on earth for sleep! Don't be found sleeping in the wrong place and or time. Don't be found sleeping during a church service, lecture or office hours. Tame sleep and then you will enjoy a great future.

As I said earlier, every area of your life requires discipline: even your appetite requires it. Don't eat just anything anywhere at anytime. Even a common one-day fasting, some young people cannot handle it! If you cannot fast while you are still single, is it when you are old that you will start learning it?

Apart from the spiritual benefits of fasting and the

fact that it is a commandment from God (Matthew 6:16), it delivers a lot of health benefits such as detoxification and much more as well. Remember Esau as a single man, sold his birthright to an undisciplined appetite (Genesis 25:29-34). Many people dig their own graves with the fork, spoon and knife through food! Your watchword should be: eat to live, not live to eat. Eat and drink in moderation.

In your appearance, be disciplined. Don't be vulgar or wild in your dressing. Be cool! Remember, you will be addressed by the way you dress.

Cultivating Character

If character is not a gift but has to be consciously cultivated, the question then is: how is character cultivated? Examine the following carefully:

Possess a Heart for God

If character is a matter of the heart, the question is where is your heart? Proverbs 23:26 says:

> **My son, give me thine heart, and let thine eyes observe my ways.**

God does not need your money, but your heart. Where is your heart? Is it towards the Word or the world? If your heart is beating towards God, His word will dwell richly, not scantily in your heart.

Let the word of Christ dwell in you richly in all wisdom; teaching and admonishing one another in psalms and hymns and spiritual songs, singing with grace in your hearts to the Lord.

Colossians 3:16

For His word to dwell richly in your heart, you must consciously put it there. The way you spend just 5 minutes in prayer and in the Word and jump out is not the way to it. What does your fellowship and communion with God as a young man or woman look like?

What you put in your heart, is what will manifest in your character, in the day of challenge. If you spend quality time in the word, it will dwell richly in your heart. Make God your priority and number one in life.

If you claim to be too busy while still single, then, when will you ever have time for God's Word? You don't have a husband or wife and you don't have children to take care of, so what is your problem? Many young people will rather spend time watching a Television show or movie than in the Word. Agreed, all those have their proper place and are not sinful in themselves, but balance is the key, for there is time for everything. There are others who spend time feeding on pornographic materials – the word cannot dwell richly in you that way! Psalms 119:11 says:

Thy word have I hid in mine heart, that I might not sin against thee.

Hide the Word in your heart. Locate what God likes and like it and whatever He hates, you too, hate it. Let the fear of God overwhelm and rule you. See how Joseph kept himself in the house of his master. Even when his master's wife was after him to lie with her, he refused to commit any act of wickedness against God. He was a man of unquestionable character because he had a heart for God. It is therefore no wonder that he was distinctively different! You are the next on the line.

Be Purpose Driven

Until you discover your purpose for living, character building might be an odious task. But when you discover purpose, it gives you a sense of direction, it gives you focus and you know, focus is power. Talking about Jesus, the Bible says in Hebrews 12:2:

Looking unto Jesus the author and finisher of our faith; who for the joy that was set before him endured the cross, despising the shame, and is set down at the right hand of the throne of God.

He endured the cross, why? He could see a crown awaiting him. Talking about Daniel, (Daniel 1:8), the Bible says that he purposed in his heart not to defile himself. He was a slave, but he must have told Himself, "Even though there are chains on my hands and feet, I know that my destiny is not chained. I purpose not to defile myself." What was his secret? Purpose! He knew where he came from and where he was going. He was confident that what he was going through was temporary, only for that point in time and would soon become history.

Purpose helps you see beyond the present to the future. Purpose is power. So, when you as a young man see others getting involved in different things that you know are contrary to God's word and are falling into character crisis, tell yourself, "I am not like others, I am different, I know where I am going. Everybody else may be doing it, but not me."

Every time I have an opportunity to speak with youths and singles, I tell them, don't follow the crowd; follow the cloud. When you follow the cloud it gives you direction and you enjoy a covering.

Be Willing to Forgive

There is no way you can cultivate a godly character if you are not armed with the willingness to forgive. What unforgiveness does is to keep you looking backwards rather than forward. Imagine someone who is driving a vehicle but keeps looking backward? For such a one, a crash is inevitable. Your destiny will not crash!

Some people even get offended at God, for whatever reason. In case you are an orphan, never sit in a corner asking, "God why did you kill my parents? All my mates get their fees paid and all their needs met; but see now, God, see what you have done to me." Don't get offended at God! If you do, who will help you?

God is your helper, not your hurter! What if the same day your parents died, you died too, what would you have done? Offence against God will negatively affect your character.

When you see others loving God and worshipping Him, never say to yourself, "They are doing that because of what He has done for them. As for me, I can't see anything He has done." If you go about with that kind of attitude, it will reflect in your relationships.

Perhaps a family member had raped you and as a result you are bitter and unforgiving towards that person. I have heard pathetic stories of how some youths and singles were raped by their uncles, cousins, neighbours and school teachers, to name a few. Some were introduced to certain terrible sexual sins such as fornication, homosexualism, pornography, masturbation, etc by close relatives.

Agreed, it's a traumatic experience! Who wants to go through such? Certainly none! I would not wish that even for my worst enemy. The pain is unimaginable! But, what has happened has happened; you can't unscramble eggs, you can't undo the incidence.

Remember, there is nothing new under the sun (Eccl. 1:9). Whatever your situation, it is common: it has happened to someone before and there is a way out of it for you (1 Corinthians 10: 13).

The reason many of such people struggle with character crisis is traceable to bitterness and unforgiveness. The good news therefore is, healing and recovery is available in Christ. Let go and let God! Take steps of faith towards your healing: accept Christ as your Lord and Savior, confess your sins, forgive and let go of the past. Jesus still heals the broken hearted today.

Even if you are a product of a broken home and your father has not proved to be responsible, don't get bitter against him. If you get bitter against him, it will reflect in your behaviour towards him and this may even make matters worse. Remember, two wrongs never make a right.

Sometime ago, a young lady came to see me for counselling. She spoke at length, and at the end of it all, I discovered that her behaviour and character were strongly influenced by her family background. She was born out of wedlock and her father's behaviour towards her mother was terrible and thereby made things worse. She was greatly embittered by her father's attitude. I made her realize the need for her to let go of the past and allow God open a new chapter of her life. Though born out of wedlock, you are not without a destiny! However, for your colourful future to unfold, forgiveness is a must. Forgiveness is a seed and whatsoever a man sows he reaps.

Matthew 6: 12 says:

And forgive us our debts, as we forgive our debtors.

When you learn to forgive others, you reap the same. Are you holding an offence against someone? Did someone mess you up, jilt or maltreat you? Let him or her go! Forgiveness may be tough, but it is not impossible. Understanding the power of forgiveness truly sets free.

Let me share a few of the fundamentals as God revealed them and enabled me to practise them in my own personal life journey.

First, understand that forgiveness is a commandment. It is a commandment from God, required for living a life of meaning. Commandments are to be obeyed, not to be debated and remember that His commandments are not grievous (1 John 5:3). They are to groom you, not to grieve you, as my husband says.

Second, forgiveness is a seed. To refuse to forgive is to be unforgiven! When you forgive others and let them go, you are forgiven and released into your destiny. Unforgiveness leads to bitterness, which ultimately embitters destiny!

Third, forgiveness is not a gift! There is no such gift as the gift of forgiveness; rather, it is a choice. It is something you have to consciously develop and walk in; go for it. Don't give room to hatred; hatred hurts the hater more than the hated, I have discovered. So, rather, choose to forgive. It is the choice of the wise!

Fourthly, Forgiveness has to be from the heart. If it is not from the heart, it is not forgiveness. Matthew 18: 35 says:

> *So likewise shall my heavenly Father do also unto you, if ye from your hearts forgive not every one his brother their trespasses.*

This explains why when you have truly forgiven someone, even when you remember the incidence and may be even see the person involved, the pain is no more there.

Finally, forgiveness brings healing. This includes healing spiritually, emotionally, mentally, psychologically and all round. Strength, health and vitality burst forth, wherever forgiveness is operational. Tensions are removed and replaced by refreshing. May this be your experience henceforth! Who is that man/woman that you are holding a grudge against? For the sake of your own self and for the betterment of your destiny, forgive and let go! Amen.

Let Go Wrong Associations

One thing is sure, show me your friends and I can predict your future. Your association has a lot to do with your character. Beware of peer pressure; as a student, don't befriend people who would want you to go about things in crooked ways. Remember,

> *The highway of the upright is to depart from evil:*
> *he that keepeth his way preserveth his soul.*
>
> Proverbs 16:17

Two cannot walk together unless they agree (Amos 3:3). Birds of a feather flock together. If your closest friend is a liar, gossip, or one that wallows in fornication and adultery, so will you.

Get Hooked to the Holy Spirit

The change in character you desire is possible with the help of the Holy Spirit. He is the agent of change. Remember that Zechariah 4:6 says:

> *Then he answered and spake unto me, saying, This*
> *is the word of the LORD unto Zerubbabel, saying,*
> *Not by might, nor by power, but by my spirit, saith*
> *the LORD of hosts.*

Developing godly character is by the help of the Spirit, not by power or might. It is not enough to be baptized in the Holy Spirit and speak in tongues; you need to constantly go to Him for help. He is your enabler and dependable helper. Wherever you have missed it, return to Him for help.

He is a person and longs for your fellowship. Don't grieve Him and don't quench Him. He is there to strengthen, energize, empower and enable you. Would you let Him?

Let me conclude this segment by sharing my personal

testimony. I gave my life to Christ early as a youth and have such a hunger for the things of God. While in secondary school, we were a group of five very close friends. We held prayer meetings, conducted Bible studies, fasted together and attended Christian meetings together. At the time, it was neither common nor normal.

Some of our classmates used to wonder the kind of persons we were then. People said things such as: "Are you the mother of God? Did you kill Jesus? Your own enthusiasm is too much!" But I was laying a solid foundation for a time to come. So, in case people are also making fun of you, never allow them distract you. Know that you are laying the foundation for your great future.

As a young man or young woman, keep your body holy. Remember that it is the temple of God (1 Corinthians 6: 19). Irrespective of the world's view and no matter how modern the world is, virginity is still scriptural. God helped me to marry as a virgin and I am not saying this with a 'more righteous than thou attitude,' but I know that, that same God can help you too – if you let Him!

One major question you should ask yourself therefore, as we round off this chapter on godly character is: what would Jesus do? Whenever you are faced with a challenge; ask yourself that question, what would Jesus do? Whatever the answer, go ahead and do it the way Jesus would have done it. Remember that He (Jesus) left us examples so we can follow in His footsteps.

The truth is, there is nothing new under the sun (Ecclesiastes 1: 9). There is no challenge you are facing as a youth or single today that others have not faced before. If they overcame, then you also can overcome. Not only can you overcome, but you shall overcome. Joseph overcame. It is your turn to overcome. Josiah overcame and he began to rule at the age of eight in the Bible. He overcame; you also shall overcome.

As you embrace character and continually cultivate, grow and strengthen it, your life shall be crises free. Character is crucial to destiny; in actual fact, it defines it. Remember your world is waiting for you! You belong to the winning camp; you shall not lose again in your life.

As this chapter closes, I leave you with this quote:

"Watch your thoughts; they become words.

Watch your words; they become actions.

Watch your actions; they become habits.

Watch your habits; they become character.

Watch your character; it becomes your destiny."

Frank Outlaw

8

MAKE WISE CHOICES

The word 'choice' means to select somebody or something selected from a number of alternatives. Without any doubt, we are creatures of choice and we make choices on a daily basis. The choices we make affect our future. Good choices enhance our future and destinies and vice versa. You must choose life in order to live. Whatever choice we make, God respects. The devil has no option than to respect our choices.

Choices are powerful and they have a lot to do with our destiny. Wrong choices can bring about ruin, while right choices bring about excellence. There is no better time to learn how to choose wisely than during the single years.

Two things to bear in mind as a single are: we live in a world of choices and you are a creature of choice. The scripture below proves this beyond any shadow of a doubt.

I call heaven and earth to record this day against you, that I have set before you life and death, blessing and cursing: therefore choose life, that both thou and thy seed may live:

Deuteronomy 30:19

God respects the choices you make

God honours the choices that you make. God will not choose for you, rather He validates your choices. In Genesis, God brought all the animals and every creature to Adam, giving him a choice to give names to all of them.

> *And out of the ground the LORD God formed every beast of the field, and every fowl of the air; and brought them unto Adam to see what he would call them: and whatsoever Adam called every living creature, that was the name thereof.*
>
> Genesis 2:19

God honoured Adam's choice of names for all animals!

Blind Bartimaeus heard about Jesus and he began to cry for mercy, saying: *"Jesus, thou son of David, have mercy upon me"*. He needed to make a choice. So, Jesus said to him, *"What do you want me to do for you?"* Meaning what is your choice? Make a choice and then I will confirm it. Mark 10:46-52, he made a choice to receive his sight and he did.

There was a woman with the issue of blood in **Matthew 9:20-22**. She had been in that condition for 12 years until, one day, she made a choice for her situation to change. She decided to touch the helm of the garment of Jesus. She said, *"if only I may but touch the helm of His garment I know I shall be made whole."* God honoured her choice and she was made whole.

Choice Is God's Gift To Man

Man is a creature of choice – his choice either makes him or breaks him, but it never leaves him neutral. Man was not made to be a robot. That is why at creation, God gave both Adam and Eve a unique gift – the power of choice. This gift was to help them succeed on the earth. As long as they could exercise it, they could choose what to do per time, when to do it, and how to do it. The most significant choice was whether to fellowship with God or not.

> *And if it seem evil unto you to serve the Lord, choose you this day whom ye will serve; whether the gods which your fathers served that were on the other side of the flood, or the gods of the Amorites, in whose land ye dwell: but as for me and my house, we will serve the Lord.*
>
> Joshua 24:15

God through the mouth of Joshua is saying here, "I give you the choice to serve Me or the gods of the land. I will not force you to serve Me. I give you that power to choose for yourself. Whatever you choose, I will honour." As you choose to honour God, He gets committed to honour you too.

If you take advantage of God's provision for sound choice making, your choices will be satisfying and valuable and you will never regret any of the choices you make. Your choices determine what happens in your life. Therefore, you have only yourself to blame for every wrong decision you make.

Information Is The Platform

The choices we make are largely determined by how informed we are. When you are well informed, you will make life-transforming choices. But, like my husband says: to be uninformed is to be deformed. If you are not well informed, the choices you make can deform your destiny. So, broaden your information base, get informed.

Before you make any choice, get necessary information on the subject matter from godly proven sources. It could be from persons or their materials, in print or electronic form such as books, magazines, tapes, CDs and so on. Ask relevant questions, if need be from appropriate sources. Seek counsel from godly counselors if necessary. Be adequately informed, so you can make quality decision.

Don't just make a choice of who to marry for example, without getting yourself well informed on the subject matter: either by listening to teachings or reading proven godly materials on it. This of course should be in addition to the manufacturer's manual on it – the Bible.

The Place Of Wisdom

The importance of the place of wisdom in making wise choices cannot be over-emphasized. Wisdom is the principal ingredient in making right choices. Proverbs 4:7 says:

> *Wisdom is the principal thing; therefore get wisdom: and with all thy getting get understanding.*

To fail a principal subject as a student is to be a principal failure! To make sound decisions, you need sound wisdom. Wisdom builds but foolishness destroys. Without wisdom, you will make foolish decisions, which will end in frustration and regrets.

Wisdom, you know, means correct application of knowledge. It is knowledge correctly acquired and applied. No one can apply or practise the knowledge that you have acquired on your behalf; you have to do it yourself.

How do I acquire this sound wisdom? You may ask. Consider the following very closely:

Settle with God's word

Psalms 119: 89 says:

> *For ever, O LORD, thy word is settled in heaven.*

When you settle with God's word, it will settle your world. Plan a daily word agenda for yourself. What physical food is to the body is what the word of God is to you. Just like no one can eat physical food on your behalf, in the same way no one can feed on God's word on your behalf. God's word is what makes wise. Psalms 119: 98 says:

> **Thou through thy commandments hast made me wiser than mine enemies: for they are ever with me.**

So, no matter how busy and tight your schedule may be, programme a daily Word agenda alongside. Let the word of wisdom dwell in you richly, not scantily. Read your Bible and anointed materials. Listen to tapes and CDs and keep filling your tank with wisdom. You never outgrow the need for the word of God. They are new every morning (Lamentation 3: 23)!

Ask The Giver

James 1: 5 says:

> **If any of you lack wisdom, let him ask of God, that giveth to all men liberally, and upbraided not; and it shall be given him.**

God is the only giver of sound wisdom. Whenever you are in need of wisdom, you can always ask Him and it shall be liberally given to you. Are you at a crossroad on certain issues right now and wondering which way to go? Pray and ask God for wisdom and it shall be given you. Personally, one of the most frequent prayers I have ever prayed has to do with wisdom.

Be praiseful

Praise is an inspiration. When you praise God from your heart, you get inspired and revelation comes; then you gain access to light from heaven, showing you which way to go. Many things in the world, situations and circumstances will want to make you murmur, grumble and complain. Rather than complain, give God praise. God praisers never lack sound wisdom.

However, you must be born again before you can access sound wisdom. Wisdom is only justified of her children (Luke 7:35). In case you have not given your life to Christ and be born again, pray the prayer at the back of this book right now with me from your heart: your life will never be the same again and thereafter you can then begin to access divine wisdom.

How Do I Choose Wisely?

The following will be of immense help to you. Come along with me and closely examine them.

Fear God

If you want to choose wisely, you must have the fear of God in your heart. In this context, the fear of God does not mean to be afraid of Him, but rather, to reverence Him and give Him His rightful place in your life. Psalms 111:10 says:

> *The fear of the LORD is the beginning of wisdom:*
> *a good understanding have all they that do his*
> *commandments.*

If you truly fear God, you will make choices that will please Him and bring Him praise and glory.

As a young man, Joseph had the fear of God and therefore made a wise choice. He refused to sleep with his master, Potiphar's wife. He saw it as wickedness and sin against God. Even though she spoke to Joseph day by day, he did not listen to her; rather, he fled for his life Genesis 39: 1- 23. At the end of the day, God vindicated Joseph distinguished him.

Samson, on the other hand, as a young man made choices that eventually ruined his enviable destiny on the laps of Delilah. He lacked the fear of God. He had been going in to harlots before he finally met Delilah.

Apart from the fact that she was an outcast with whom Samson should not have related, Delilah had deceived him several times. Yet he chose to remain with her. Finally, Samson was captured by his enemies, his eyes were plucked out and he was subjected to humiliation before his final demise (Judges 16:1-3). It was a tragic end.

The fear of God made the difference between the decisions made by the two men we have considered. Now, the choice is yours. Whose example will you choose to emulate?

Be Futuristic

Look beyond the present into the future, when making decisions. See beyond now to the later. Many youth and singles are short sighted in their choices. When sin stares you in the face, enticing you and presenting itself to be pleasurable, remember that afterwards, it bites like a serpent. The pleasure of sin is just for a moment; beware (Hebrews 11:25).

As a single lady, what are you doing running around with a married man who is your father's age, or with a single man who is not your husband? You single man, what are you looking for taking a woman that is not your wife? Why should you take her to bed?

Take this from me: one night of delight can lead to a lifetime of disaster! The choices you make today can and definitely will affect your future. This explains why you have to be very careful about the decisions you make.

A wise man once said, "Wise people choose today what will make them happy tomorrow. Foolish people choose today only what will make them happy today." How far you go in life is therefore a product of your choices.

If only you can catch a picture of your future, you will make wise choices with ease; your prevailing circumstances not withstanding. Though in the land of captivity, Daniel as a young man chose not to defile himself because he had a clear picture of his glorious future (Daniel 1: 8).

Hebrews 12:2 says:

> *Looking unto Jesus the author and finisher of our faith; who for the joy that was set before him endured the cross, despising the shame, and it set down at the right hand of the throne of God.*

Jesus, our perfect example, despised the shame, pain and the agony on the cross, because He could see the crown that was set before Him. He was futuristic in His choice, which eventually brought salvation to mankind. We are to follow in His footsteps.

The true picture of your future is in the word of God, but you have to search it out! If you catch this picture, nothing can stop you from making wise choices and nothing can take your joy. You should be excited. You should refuse to cast your head down or look pitiable. Joseph demonstrated this in practical terms (Genesis

40:7). You know, joy is one of the fruits of the spirit.

Disconnect From Your Negative Past

To make wise choices in life, you must consciously disconnect from your negative past. The negative past is one of the greatest traps that the devil puts on the path of believers, especially youths, in causing them to make foolish choices. Some people tend to think that since they made wrong, foolish choices before, for which they are suffering serious consequences; the choices they make now would make no difference anyway. They live in their past and therefore never lay hold on their great future. That is the devil's lie.

No matter how terrible your past may be, you can turn over a new leaf and face the future with great hope, by making right choices. Could a man's past be more terrible than that of Saul turned Paul, who later became the chiefest of the Apostles? Acts 8: 1; 9:1-2.

Never allow your past to imprison your future! Agreed, you have made wrong choices in the past that have affected your life negatively; but the good news is that God is not judging you by your past (Isaiah 43:18-19). All you need do now is, be born again, repent of your sins and call on God for mercy, so He can wash you with his precious blood. Forsake your old ways, and totally follow Him from now on, by following His word.

Begin to make choices bearing the picture of your great future in mind. Even the sky will not be your limit. Someone has said, if the devil reminds you of your negative past, you remind him of his devastating future!

Make The Holy Spirit Your Principal Guide

We live in a wild wicked world. To successfully journey through it unhurt, a dependable guide is required. The Holy Spirit is our master guide. This explains why John 16:13 says:

> *Howbeit when he, the Spirit of truth, is come, he will guide you into all truth: for he shall not speak of himself; but whatsoever he shall hear, that shall he speak: and he will shew you things to come.*

The Holy Spirit is not just to make us speak in tongues; whilst speaking in tongues, is the only certified evidence of baptism in the Holy Spirit, his mission includes that of guidance.

Before you make choices, contact the Holy Spirit, give him room; involve him by speaking in tongues and waiting to hear him guide you. If you are about to take a decision and having prayed in tongues intensely; if there is no liberty of release in your spirit, you require caution. It may be a check, for where the Spirit of the Lord is, there is liberty (2 Corinthians 3:17; Acts 20:22).

Any decision you are making and you feel bound in the spirit, God is not in it. Wisdom demands that you abandon such with speed. I practise this regularly in my life, and I can tell you it works!

In case you are born again, but not yet baptized in the Holy Spirit, with the evidence of speaking in tongues, right now where you are, from your heart, call on Jesus, the baptizer to baptize you; open your mouth and begin to give God thanks and I can assure you that you will begin to speak in tongues. It's that simple! Thereafter, begin to engage the Holy Spirit in your decision-making processes.

The Instrument of Choice

Every human being has a God-given instrument that enables him to make choices in life. Without this very important instrument, you will certainly be overwhelmed by so many issues; major and minor, awaiting your decision on a daily basis. The mind is this priceless instrument.

The state of a man's mind determines the quality of his choices, which ultimately determines the quality of his life. If there is any area of your life that you need to work on very diligently, so as to ensure that you obtain excellent results, it is improving the quality of your mind.

For example, as a young lady or young man, there are many schools to choose from per time. Yet before you gain admission into one, you had to engage your mind. You checked through the brochure of some institutions to find out if the course of your dream is being offered, whether the location of the school is satisfactory to you or not, etc.

You make your choice and live with the consequences of that choice – whether for good or evil. God does not make choices for anyone. You make your choice by engaging your God-given instrument, your mind. God has given you a regenerated mind, so you can give Him rest. The truth is that, if you sharpen your mind appropriately, it will be easy for you to make godly choices that will give you joy, peace and rest.

The question then is, how do I get my mind adequately sharpened?

Sharpening Your Mind

New birth: 1 Corinthians 2:16 says:

...But we have the mind of Christ.

New birth guarantees you access to the mind of Christ. In other words, when you get born again, one of the gifts of God you receive at salvation is the gift of the mind of Christ. As far as God is concerned, no matter how much of a dummy you were before salvation, now you have access to the mind of His Son, you can tap into that rich deposit and begin to reason at the same frequency as Christ.

If you read through the Gospel of Matthew, Mark, Luke and John, you will discover that Jesus Christ never made a wrong choice. If you have His mind therefore, you cannot continue making wrong choices. Redemption has excluded you from the plaque of wrong choices – choices that you ever live to regret.

Now that you have the mind of Christ, as you productively engage it, it will produce treasures that will lead to your triumph in Jesus name.

Mind Renewal: Read this scripture very carefully with me aloud.

> *Therefore, I urge you, brothers, in view of God's mercy, to offer your bodies as living sacrifices, holy and pleasing to God – this is your spiritual act of worship. Do not conform any longer to the pattern of this world, but be transformed by the renewing of your mind.*
>
> *Then you will be able to test and approve what God's will is – His good, pleasing and perfect will.*
>
> Romans 12:1-2 (NIV)

At new birth, you have the mind of Christ, that is clear; but for you to get the results that Christ will get if He were in your situation today, you will have to renew your mind daily with the Word of God. How do you renew your mind?

Study and meditate on the Word: The Word of God is quick and powerful, it is able to penetrate deep into the thoughts and intents of the heart; it is able to locate the soul and enable it to make informed choices.

The Bible says in *2 Timothy 2:15:*

> *Study to shew thyself approved unto God, a workman that needeth not to be ashamed, rightly dividing the Word of truth.*

As you study and meditate on the Word of God, you are rubbing minds with the mind of God. God is the only wise God, so when His Word dwells richly in you, you cannot make foolish choices in life.

> *This book of the law shall not depart from thy mouth; but thou shalt meditate therein day and night, that thou mayest observe to do according to all that is written therein; for then thou shalt make thy way prosperous, and then thou shalt have good success.*
>
> Joshua 1:8

As you meditate and confess the Word of God, the power of God is also being released to transform every area of your life, including your thinking pattern.

Ask for Wisdom: *James 1:5* makes it clear that,

> *If any of you lack wisdom, let him ask of God, that*

giveth liberally, and upbraideth not; and it shall be
given him.

Wisdom is a key ingredient in making right choices, as I said earlier; every man who has a wise heart ends up making right decisions. Now God says in His Word that if you lack this key ingredient, you should ask of Him that gives it generously and without controversy and you will receive it. Are you faced with confusing decisions? Why don't you ask God to give you the wisdom to make the right choice? As you do, I see God come to your help today.

Rub minds with similar and/or superior minds: You can polish your mind by interacting with superior minds. Listen to them; watch them make choices and take actions; ask questions on why they made certain choices; learn from their mistakes; seek sincere advice on the demanding issues of your life. These are all ways of rubbing your mind for effective sharpening and right choices will be the end result. The Bible speaking says:

Wise friends make you wise, but you hurt yourself
by going around with fools. Just as iron sharpens
iron, friends sharpen the minds of each other.
Proverbs13:20; 27: 17 (CEV)

Interacting with similar/superior minds could be through direct interpersonal relationships, reading books, listening to tapes or any other means of communication, impartation or any other avenue of connection.

Live a life of appreciation: The scripture says:

> *For although they knew God, they glorified Him not as God nor gave thanks to Him, but their THINKING became futile and their foolish HEARTS were darkened.*
>
> Romans 1:21 (NIV)

The reverse of the scripture above is also true: if a man would give glory to God, he will not only become fruitful, successful and resourceful in his thinking, but also judicious and discreet in his heart. The cheapest way to get God to baptize you with the spirit of wisdom is to keep appreciating Him for every 'little' act of His in your life.

If you thank Him for the one He did yesterday, you provoke Him to do for you greater and bigger miracles today. Wisdom is available with Him, but He will not give it to the ungrateful. Now stop complaining and start praising Him and watch His mighty hand rest on your mind, giving you tremendous entrance into the hidden things of life.

Proof of Right Choices

But, how do I know whether I have made right or wrong

choices? You may ask. Good question. The following are some of the characteristics to watch out for:

Peace: Right choices are usually accompanied with peace (Psalms 25:12-13; 23:1-end).

Joy: When you are on the right path decision-wise, you experience unexplainable joy (Hebrews 12: 2).

Divine Strength: Supernaturally, you get energized when you make correct choices. No matter what the outcome of the decision demands, there is strength to match the task (Judges 6:14).

From this day forward, concerning every area of your life, career, business, health, relationships and your future, there shall be no more regret! I pray that the blood of Jesus Christ will wash away every wrong choice you have made in the past. I pray that God will give you His grace from this day forward to make right choices in the name of Jesus Christ! It is done!

9
Chapter 9

BUILD SOUND RELATIONSHIPS

He that walketh with wise men shall be wise: but a companion of fools shall be destroyed

Proverbs 13: 20

Relationships are vital to destiny. Your association defines your destination. The relationships you are into never leave you the same; they either add to you or take away from you. They either increase you or decrease you.

Relationships are powerful and we get involved in them at one level or another on a daily basis. The scriptural understanding of how to build and keep sound, healthy and Godly relationships is very vital in the fulfillment of destiny.

One of the very core areas that affect singles a great deal is in relationships. The best time to begin building sound, healthy, strong and meaningful relationships is when you are still single. Therefore, it is very important for you to read this chapter very carefully and be sure to apply the issues to your day-to-day living.

I see God releasing grace for you to depart from every unhealthy relationship and He will guide your steps into only relationships that will move you forward. You will go forward!

To 'relate' means to connect. It means to contact and interact. To relate means to link up with something or with somebody. To relate means to be involved in or with; to connect, to interact, to link up and to be involved in. Therefore, relationships can be defined as the way in which two or more people connect.

A sound relationship is one that is free from defect, decay, damage. It is a relationship in good condition. It is unshakeable, healthy and valid. These are the kind of relationships that God expects you to get involved in.

Why Relationships?

In order for you to build relationships that will positively influence your life, you must have a full knowledge of the reasons why God wants us to be involved in relationships. There are two basic things that you must understand here:

First, God is relational in nature.

The Bible says:

> *For there are three that bear record in heaven, the Father, the Word, and the Holy Ghost: and these*

three are one.

1 John 5:7

There is a powerful relationship between the Godhead, the Father, the Son and the Holy Spirit. The Bible says that these three are one. That is, they agree in one. This is a vivid picture of God's relational nature.

In the Garden of Eden, God related well with Adam before the fall of man. Out of His relationship with him, God knew that Adam would need a helpmeet for the work in the garden and for companionship. Also on the day that they ate the forbidden fruit, He came in the cool of the day to see to their welfare. God believes in relationships and He Himself is into strong relationships. If He is relational then, it is necessary for us to also get involved.

Second, Man is created to relate.

In *Genesis 1:27*, the Bible says:

So God created man in his own image, in the image of God created he him; male and female created he them.

Man is created in the image of God, therefore he is expected to relate and connect. Nobody can ever live successfully in isolation. We all need one another. You need people to help you get to where you are going in life, no matter what level you are. You cannot live in an Island of your own, no matter who you are.

Every part of the body work and relate together (Ephesians 4:16), so also you are created to relate. In actual fact, man is created to be inter-dependent and that includes you. God made man to *"...dwell together..."* (Psalms 133:1).

As a matter of fact, you are a product of relationships. The relationship between your father and your mother is what resulted in your birth. I therefore believe it is very important for us to know the different types of relationships and how to successfully build them.

Types Of Relationships

Basically, there are two types of relationships. The first is your relationship with God while the second is with your fellow men. Let's briefly examine each of them.

Relationship With God

Your relationship with God can be considered from three different levels, namely: as your creator, father and Lord.

God is your Creator (Genesis 1:27) and you can relate with Him as His creature. To every human being on planet earth, born again or not, whether it is accepted by them or not, God created everyone. So, He is the creator of every living.

God becomes your Father when you give your life to

Jesus, and get born again.

> *But as many as received him, to them gave he power*
> *to become the sons of God, even to them that believe*
> *on his name:*

John. 1:12

When you have a personal relationship and encounter with Him, then He becomes your Father. He is now both your creator and your Father.

However, the highest relationship with God is when He becomes your Lord. He becomes your Lord when your life is sown as a seed in dedication and absolute commitment unto Him. He is only the Lord of those who have consciously, deliberately dedicated their lives unto Him. Those who are ready to say: 'yes Lord' to His will, plan, purpose, and destiny. Those who are ready to say like Apostle Paul: *"For me to live is Christ and to die is gain"* (Philipians 1:21). This is the level that God desire from every one of us. You graduate from one level to another, in that order.

The question then is: is He Lord over your life? Or are you lord over yourself? He can be your Father without being your Lord. But when He becomes your Lord, you can be sure nothing can change His plan and purpose for your life. May that be your portion in Jesus' name.

It is very important for you therefore, to understand

that God desires an intimate relationship with you. He wants you to have an intimate relationship with Him, but you have to open up to Him.

To Develop an Intimate relationship with God, however, you have to consciously, deliberately, intentionally, willingly, excitedly make yourself available through deep word study, prayer life and constant fellowshipping with Him.

There is no other relationship in life that compares in value, equal or can replace your relationship with God. In actual fact, we can safely say that your relationship with God is the only sure foundation for success in every other kind of relationship. It is utterly important for you to straighten up your relationship with God.

How you treat God without any doubt, will affect how you treat men. How do you treat God? Do you respect Him or you are one of those that take him for granted? Do you see your relationship with Him as one of those things just to fulfill righteousness? You must relate with Him with a deeper knowledge of who He is. It's time therefore, to seek God and search for Him whole-heartedly! Seek Him and search for Him with all your heart, because that is the foundation. Remember, He says in His Word, only those who seek Him early shall find Him (Proverbs 8:17).

Word Study: The Bible is the written word of God. It is as powerful as if you are hearing God speak to you audibly. Know God personally and daily develop your relationship with Him through deep word study. Studying His word will make you familiar with his voice. Naturally, if you have a strong relationship with someone, like a family member or a close friend, you could easily pick his or her voice among the crowd.

One time, many years ago when my biological mother was still alive; we went to a particular city for a meeting. It was such a great crowd it was an uphill task for us to get back in the car after the event. But in the midst of the mammoth crowd, I could identify my mother's voice; even though I never knew that she was in that city at that point in time. That is how it should be with God. This kind of relationship can be developed through your studying of His word. If you are familiar with God's voice, He will caution and deliver you from entering wrong relationships with men.

Prayer Life: Prayer is our communication link with God. If your prayer life is buoyant, then your relationship with Him will be buoyant. God desires that we commune with Him daily. Just as it is not natural for you to have a relationship with someone you do not talk to, so also you cannot have a deep relationship with God if your prayer life is not sound.

Psalms 65:2 says:

> *O thou that heareth prayer unto thee shall all flesh come.*

God, who is your father, is ready to hear you anytime you call. Do not hesitate to commune with Him even concerning the minutest details of your life.

Constant Fellowship: The gathering together of saints in fellowship is a vital way of relating with God. Go to church regularly, it strengthens your relationship with God. Refuse to be only a Sunday, Sunday worshiper. God is always there whenever and wherever His name is called upon in truth and in deed.

> *For where two or three are gathered together in my name, there am I in the midst of them.*
>
> Matthew 18:20

As you go to church and attend fellowship, you also partake of the gifts that operate in the body of Christ and you are more rooted in your relationship with your heavenly father.

Relationship With Men

The second type of relationships is your relationship with men. The word 'men' here is not talking about gender. This is not referring to the male gender of God's creation. 'Men' in this content is referring to both male and female gender of God's creation. Here, I am referring to your relationships with people.

This is in three levels: your superiors, mates and juniors. During your life's journey, you will definitely meet and need people in these three categories and this is the best time to develop such relationships.

Your superior: Who is your superior? Your superiors are the people you draw from. They could be your boss at work, your lecturers in the school or your spiritual parents. These people have the skill you do not have, the experience you do not have and you could climb on their shoulder so as to see ahead. The truth is: no matter your level in life right now, there are and there will always be, people above you. These are people who can speak into your life, especially when the going seems to get tough.

My husband and I and indeed my entire household, are beneficiaries of this type of relationships. During the time I went through the valley of the shadow of death, this was one of the major areas of strength for me. Senior men in ministry were greatly used of God to stand in the gap, to ensure my total liberty and freedom from the pangs of death and alleluia, today I am a living testimony and can boldly say that God is too faithful to fail, He is dependable and He is more than enough!

Be humble and smart enough to identify them and draw from their wealth of knowledge and experience, to expedite your rate of accomplishment in life.

Your mates: These are either your colleagues at work, in school or people at the level that you are. These are the people you share with. They could be your friends. Water always seeks its own level and birds of a feather flock together. The need for you to identify your own company (Acts 4:23) so as to derive maximum benefits from it, cannot be over-emphasized. Remember, if you stand alone, you fall alone. One tree never makes a forest!

Then, **Your Juniors:** These are the people that you flow out to, the ones that look up to you as their superior. Wisdom demands that you identify people that you can reach out to. Water easily flows down hills!

The need to build sound relationships with people at these levels cannot be over-emphasized. No matter whom you are or the categories to which you belong, you should get involved in these three levels of relationships. You will always have superiors, mates and juniors. The wisdom to build these strongly, may you receive it today.

Fundamental Factors:

To build sound and meaningful relationships, certain fundamental factors must be in place. Let us examine some of them here.

Define the purpose

This is the principal factor that must be in place, if a sound relationship must be built. To every thing under the sun, including relationships, there is a purpose (Ecclesiastes 3:1). Whatever relationship you are into, whether with your mates; superiors; or juniors, it is crucial and fundamental to define the purpose of it, right from the outset.

Dr Myles Munroe said, *"When purpose is not known, abuse in inevitable."* Many people abuse relationships at different levels because of lack of clearly defined purpose. You should ask yourself: "Why am l into this relationship? What do I hope to achieve by this relationship? Is it to achieve a common goal? Is it educational? Or is it to end up in marriage?" Purpose is power and relationships thrive on it. Purpose enhances your focus.

Constantly keep the purpose of your relationship before you. Always remember what brought you together in the first place. For instance, what attracted you to each other spiritually, physically and mentally in the first instance?

Defining and knowing the purpose of your relationship, will help you to fight and overcome distractions. With well-defined purpose, you are able to know whether you are on track or not. It makes correct evaluation possible. Several people make a shipwreck of their faith and end up in ungodly relationships for lack of clearly defined purpose.

Be Sincere to yourself

Another major factor is that you must know, understand and be true to yourself. Remember, you are the principal actor in any relationship you are involved in. So, refuse to play the game of self-deceit! Many people are strangers to themselves. The truth is that they do not know their strength and area of weakness. They never find out in the first place. They keep falling over the same mistakes and keep on going into wrong hands. Know, understand and be true to yourself.

Where knowledge is present, power is present for performance. Where there is understanding, there will be outstanding accomplishments. There are many people who don't understand themselves and relationships that they are into. For any relationship to be outstanding, a good understanding is required. If you find it difficult to relate with yourself, you will not have a successful relationship with others.

Be practical, be real! Find out your weaknesses and your strength, attitude and temperament. Pay attention to your behaviour. Do not play careless with your life; you don't have a spare one. Interestingly, there is no return match in the game of life; there is no replacement for the current one you have. Handle it with care! Those who live carelessly end up in careless relationships, thereby making a shipwreck of their faith.

To build sound and meaningful relationships, learn to seek and receive help in your area of weakness.

1 Corinthians 10:12 says:

> *Wherefore let him that thinketh he standeth take heed lest he fall.*

Successful relationships begin with you. Do not hide from your own flesh. Do not pretend to be super-strong when you know you are not. A sound relationship is possible when the principal actor, which is you, is sincere.

Examine your motives

Motive is defined as the reason for doing something. Motives are powerful and it is everything. No wonder 2 Corinthians 13:5 says:

> *Examine yourselves, whether ye be in the faith: prove your own selves: know ye not your own selves, how that Jesus Christ is in you, except ye be reprobates?*

Whatever relationships you get yourself involved in, ask yourself this simple question: is my motive pure? Is my motive right? Is my motive righteous? Is my motive godly? Impure motives will produce impure relationships. Examine your motives; you are the best examiner of your life whether there is an ulterior motive or whether your motive is pure and godly. Your motive is clearly known and never hidden to you.

Amazingly, some people go into relationships and try to act right but with impure motives. They engage themselves in the game of self-deceit, attempting to cover up and pretending to be who they are not. Such people have forgotten that their motives will soon betray them. It is like attempting to hide behind one finger, it never works!

What are your motives in the relationships you are into right now? Young man, you invited that lady for a dinner, but your motive was to take advantage of her. You single and influential lady, you probably gave that brother a lift the other day, but your motive was to have immoral acts with him! Check it out

It is possible, for example, for a man to invite a lady for dinner whereas his motive is to rape her. A lady, for instance, could pursue a man for marriage, but her motive could be because of the fame, name and material wealth that he possesses. If you are into any relationship with an impure motive, the earlier you quit the better for you, if you do not want to endanger your destiny. Beware of your motive!

Interestingly, God sees beyond your actions to your motives. You may succeed in deceiving man, but can you deceive

God? Impossible! So, right from the outset, sanitize your motive before you enter into any relationship whatsoever; it will make it sound, healthy and rewarding.

Be a contributor

It is very important for you to enter a relationship as a contributor and not a burden. What you take into a relationship will determine what you get out of it. Whether it is a relationship with your superior, your mates or your junior; or whether it is even a relationship for getting into marriage: what you get and what you find in that relationship has a lot to do with what you put into it.

Take a close look at Proverbs 27:17:

> *Iron sharpeneth iron; so a man sharpeneth the countenance of his friend.*

Seek to sharpen, add something to the life of the other party or parties involved in that relationship. Don't keep looking for what to get, what to grab, what to take, what to benefit. Instead, think of what to add and give. Constantly bear in mind the fact that what you make happen for others determines what God makes happen for you.

Giving, you must remember is living! So, give, contribute and invest spiritually, materially and otherwise to the development and growth of the relationships you are involved in; stop being a critic. What contributions have brought into the relationship you are in right now? What contributions have you ever made or are you willing to make? Think about this for a moment. When contribution is one-sided, it cripples relationships.

Sometime back, a young man came to me for counsel. He was into a relationship with a lady and both of them intended to get married. However, the relationship became unstable and they were having problems. In the course of the discussion, I discovered that one of the major problem areas had to do with the fact that contribution was one sided in that relationship. He on his own part contributed spiritually and otherwise. He constantly prayed, gave gifts, showed concern and the like while the other party did not. Well, eventually they had to break up.

Beware of selfishness! Stop taking undue advantage of people. Refuse to join the company of those who keep sucking life out of others, rather than adding to them. Don't always sit at the receiving end in a relationship.

Communicate Effectively

Every sound relationship thrives on good

communication. Assumption in relationships could be very dangerous. My husband says humorously, assumption is the mother of frustration! Do not assume anything, speak out, and find out the things in the mind of the people you are into relationships with. What do they think about you? This will help you clear a wrong impression that the other party might be having.

Sometimes, lack of good communication has truncated a good and well meaning relationship. A closed mouth could lead to a closed destiny. Remember that no one is a mind reader. Communicate effectively and you will set the stage for a sound relationship.

Researchers say that we spend 70% of our waking time communicating and 30% of our communication is talking. Keep in mind the fact that no matter what you do, you have to speak to one person or another on a daily basis. You therefore need to learn how to speak correctly. The scripture says in Ephesians 4:29

Let no corrupt communication proceed out of your mouth.

For this to be so, you need to allow God to touch your mouth with the coal of fire, giving no room to the adversary!

For communication to be effective however, it must involve a two sided stimulating conversation. Very importantly: no communication must be allowed to degenerate into arguments! This is because arguments put you farther apart.

There are different purpose of communication, but I will briefly mention four here. First, communication can be for information. This involves giving of necessary information to the one you are relating with. This is crucial especially because it could be very dangerous to assume what you don't know.

The second purpose of communication is fellowship. This type of communication involves sharing, it frees from loneliness. Then, you have the problem solving form of communication. This is used to handle any specific problematic situation that may be on ground.

Lastly, there is the fact finding form of communication which involves asking relevant questions. Remember, only those who ask questions are entitled to answers!

Personally, I use a combination of these types of communication, depending on the situation at hand per time. Over the years, this has helped me in no small measure in building sound relationships since the time I was single. Even now that I have been married over twenty- five (25) years, I still engage communication for these purposes. Sometimes, when my husband preaches and makes reference to some instances that I could not remember, at a later date and right time, I ask him and he explains.

Understand however, that correct timing is crucial to good communication. It is possible to say the right thing at the wrong time! It is said that most of the friction in communication is caused by one of these: wrong timing (when), wrong setting (where) or wrong manner (tone, how).

You probably will know how many different meanings the little phrase "no, nothing's wrong" can have, depending on who's saying it! But what is important is to ask if you are not sure what he or she means and speak honestly and openly so that the miscommunication is avoided in the first place.

Never keep a feeling bottled up because you are afraid it is not what your friend wants to hear or because you worry about sounding silly. And, you know, if you need some time to think something through before you are ready to talk about it, the right person will definitely give you some space to do that if you ask for it.

Engage in Constant Evaluation

Constantly evaluate your relationships. In evaluating your relationships, ask yourself: is this relationship profitable, both to me and to the other person or persons involved? Is it contributing anything to me

SINGLE WITH A DIFFERENCE

and the parties involved? Ask yourself questions such as: Is it adding anything to me or is it constantly sapping me? Is it leaving me refreshed, energized or is it draining me. Any relationship you are into that keeps draining you is leading you to the grave faster than you thought.

In a sound relationship, there will always be mutual respect for each other. This means that each person values who the other is. You need to evaluate whether this respect is there or not and if it is, whether it is growing or diminishing.

Another important area that requires constant evaluation is trust. No relationship at any level for that matter can be healthy without trust. Evaluate whether there is trust and if it is present, whether it is growing or not.

Talking about love, I have heard some people, especially singles, say that love is blind! Nothing can be farther from the truth, because God is love (1 John 4:8) and God is not blind! Open your eyes wide and don't allow any fantasy and emotion to mislead you.

Any relationship that is taking you away from the realities of life and leaves you only in a dreamland of fantasy is neither a sound nor a godly one. Is your relationship moving you forward or drawing backward?

Examine your spiritual walk with God because any

relationship with man at any level, male or female that draws you backward in your walk with God is not godly and does not deserve your consideration or attention.

Relationship With The Opposite Sex

Now, one very vital aspect of relationships that I want to discuss here is the one with the opposite sex. From creation, there has been the male and female gender of God's creation. Genesis 1:27 says:

So God created man in his own image, in the image of God created he him; male and female created he them.

There is no separate male and female world. God created both male and female to co-exist. It is important to know how to relate profitably with the opposite sex, especially in this wicked world.

Here, I want to share some power ingredients for godly relationship with the opposite sex with you. I have seen them work in the lives of many youths, singles and even married people and I know they will work for you as well if you apply them to your life.

Understand male and female differences: First, you must understand male and female differences. God made us male and female without mistakes (Genesis 1:27). Your understanding of these differences will help you to relate reasonably. As male and female, He created us not to compete with each other, but to complement each other.

You must have heard this slogan: 'what a man can do, a woman can do.' Nothing can be farther from the truth than this. It is not scriptural. There are several things a man can do that a woman cannot do. For example, a woman cannot father a child. In the same vein, there are many things a woman can do that a man cannot do: a man cannot mother a child. So, there is no point competing.

God didn't create us for competition as male and female, He created us for complementation! If you have the understanding of this powerful principle, you will live your life in peace, blessings and quietness. Understand male and female differences.

There are certain things that can turn a man on emotionally, but would not necessarily turn a woman on and vice versa. For instance, women are turned on by what they hear, while men are turned on with what they see. As a man, when you relate with women of opposite sex, be cautious of what you say. Do not speak deceitfully, irresponsibly or dirty language. As a woman, be cautious of the way you dress and appear before men, because they are turned on with their sight.

When you dress and expose your nakedness, it is a sign of irresponsibility; you sell yourself cheap and it erodes your dignity. Wisdom demands that you stay clear from clothes that are revealing. Remember that your 'private parts' should be kept private. Do not set a trap for people with your careless dressing. Do not constitute yourself into a stumbling block or a death trap for others! In addition, the way you dress will determine how you will be addressed.

The way you dress portrays the state of your mind. A man that was once possessed with evil spirit met Jesus and was completely delivered. Thereafter, he was found sitting at the feet of Jesus, clothed and in his right mind (Mark 5:15; Luke 8:35). People in their right minds always reflect this in their dressing. A good understanding of this will help you to make a success of such relationships. Many mighty men and women have fallen because they either lacked understanding of this or this knowledge is not properly handled.

When some people see improperly dressed individuals, especially of the opposite sex, they start having some motions in the flesh, which if not quickly arrested, could lead to a major catastrophe. Before you know it, a very great and powerful giant, an inventor had fallen flat on the laps of another Delilah.

Set boundaries: This factor is very necessary especially when you are dealing with the opposite sex. Whether with your superior, mate or junior, you must set your boundaries. Any relationship that has no boundaries, will surely hit the rock! Define the 'no-go' areas. Keep yourself pure (I Timothy 4:12). Remember, you can live pure even in this impure world.

Even in relating with people of the same sex, there has to be boundaries. This is certainly a requirement if you must be positively different as a single. The issue of homosexuality and child rape is creeping fast into the Church these days. So there have to be boundaries.

Even for parents, whether your children are of the same or different sex, it is necessary to set boundaries. A time comes when your children should not keep seeing each other's nakedness any more.

Relationships defer and they are in levels. But these boundaries must answer these four questions: Where, What, When and How.

In relating with somebody of the opposite sex, you must be able to set boundaries of **where** you and that individual can be found and where you must never be found. That talks about places and locations. Whether it's a relationship with your superior, mate, or junior, you must define the limit of where you can go or be found together.

When you are together, ask yourself the question: 'What am I doing with this individual here'? You must of a necessity define what you could do, as well as, what you must not be found doing with a person of the opposite sex. What part of your body an opposite sex must never be allowed to touch! Sounds funny? This is crucial! Remember, God gave you sense so that you can give him rest!

Then, talking about timing, you know that there is time for everything under the sun (Eccl. 3:1). It is crucial to set boundaries concerning when it is safe for you, to be found with someone of the opposite sex and what time is not. You must set rules for yourself in life, because it is only those who obey rules that end up as rulers.

Also, remember that your comportment matters a lot. You must also decide how you must never be found with an opposite sex. How you present yourself will determine the respect you will command in any form of relationship you are into.

You should not be seen in compromising situations with an opposite sex. For example, you open the door to the devil when you are found in the dark at odd times in secluded places with an opposite sex.

You cannot claim to be holding an all-night prayer meeting behind closed doors, alone with someone of an opposite sex; no matter how 'spiritual' you may be. You will be setting a death trap for yourself by so doing, no matter the kind of relationship between you!

Even, when you sit in the midst of people of opposite sex, wisdom demands that you do not sit in a manner that will expose your privacy. Don't be careless! Your life is too precious. You don't have a spare one, handle it with care. Your destiny shall not be destroyed!

Singles: flee the forbidden fruit which is pre-marital sex. Keep your sex drive in neutral. Keep your sexual appetite under control. Remember that your memory will not be as kind to you as God!

Beware of un-edifying complements: Un-edifying complements have sent several people to the grave in ungodly relationship. Mind you, compliments in themselves are good but they must be used sensibly. When you give complements, be honest and let your motive be pure. Do not give compliment to flatter. Never allow compliments from people, make you to over-estimate yourself.

When someone of the opposite sex keeps giving un-edifying complements about your person, dressing, appearance and the like, especially when it is coming from the same person always it could suggest danger. The faster you run away from him or her, the better for your life and destiny.

The Bible says:

For the lips of a strange woman drop as an

honeycomb, and her mouth is smoother than oil:

Proverbs 5:3

Remember, there are strange women as well as strange men!

Be sensitive and sensible: In relating with the opposite sex, you must be very sensitive as well as sensible. To be sensible refers to your ability to make good judgments whereas to be sensitive refers to how much you are aware of things or other people.

The scripture says in Proverbs 22:3:

> *A prudent man foreseeth the evil, and hideth himself: but the simple pass on, and are punished.*

Be watchful and receptive to spiritual signals. Let your spiritual antenna be on at all times. When you receive a signal from God that a relationship is dangerous and you find out that you lack peace, as a sensible person, you should put a stop to that relationship.

If you have a troubled feeling concerning any relationship, or you start feeling uncomfortable, whenever a particular person of the opposite sex is around you, or you start having unholy motions of the flesh, it may be a pointer to the fact that danger is at the door!

Every immoral act stems from such unholy motions of the flesh, not properly handled. You may need to make a u-turn so that your destiny will not be torn into pieces. It may be a signal that there is fire on the mountain and you may need to run for your life.

It is your responsibility to abstain, shrink and keep away from every appearance of evil in whatever form or whatever kind it may be (I Thesselonians 5:22). As you do that, He leads you in the right direction and this will sharpen your spiritual antenna.

Be open to correction: Correction simply refers to a change that makes something more accurate than it was before. Corrections are part and parcel of life. In relating with the opposite sex, you must be open to corrections, especially when they are Bible based. The bible says:

> *Correction is grievous unto him that forsaketh the way: and he that hateth reproof shall die.*
>
> Proverbs 15:10

As this chapter comes to a conclusion, it is important for me to clearly state here that there are lots of benefits that you stand to enjoy, when you engage in sound relationships at the three different levels – with your superiors, mates and juniors. The scripture says:

> *...in all labour there is profit...*
>
> Proverbs 14:23

This means that in all sound and godly relationships, there is profit. These benefits are amazing and cover different areas of life. Let us briefly examine some of them here.

Benefits Of Relationships

It makes life smooth

What engine oil is to a car is what sound relationships are to life. They lubricate your destiny and help you function optimally. The better part of you comes out and your performance is positively enhanced.

Speedy Accomplishment

You stand the chance of getting things accomplished faster and better. Sweeping with a broomstick for example, can never give you the same effect as sweeping with a bunch of it, as far as effectiveness and speed is concerned (Luke 10:17). You must have heard the phrase: "one tree never makes a forest". Your effectiveness is enhanced by sound relationships.

Release of Potentials

When you are involved in sound, godly relationships, you stand a chance of viewing things from different perspectives and even engage in exchange of profitable ideas. Remember that iron sharpens iron (Proverbs 27:17). As you rub minds together on various issues of life, your mind is sharpened. This in turn makes for innovations and release of your hidden potentials. You are then able to make better impact as well as improve and maintain relevance. This eventually makes for a better you, bringing about fulfillment of destiny.

Joy of Involvement

The fact that you are profitably involved in the lives of others brings joy, especially when you see such people making progress and impact in life. Personally, it gladdens my heart when I see people that I associate with making impact, moving forward, breaking new grounds and having testimonies.

Of course, who wants to associate with the stagnated? I certainly don't! Or do you? I know you don't! Let it excite you, not depress you, when you see the people you relate with, making progress. Keep in mind the fact that whatever you love and are excited about, you naturally attract and vice versa.

Some people are never happy seeing others that they relate with make progress in life. This is ungodly and very dangerous. In actual fact, if you are relating with anyone who is neither interested nor excited in your progress in life, you need to get out of that relationship fast, irrespective of whatever kind of level of relationship it might be, whether it is with your superior, mate or junior.

You are strengthened

There is power in togetherness! This explains why the scripture says two are better than one (Ecclesiastes 4:9-10). You are constantly inspired to keep on. Rather than get weary, especially in the face of challenges, you are strengthened and encouraged to forge ahead. This in turn helps you to easily overcome obstacles and challenges of life.

These benefits and more I enjoyed during my single years and even now over twenty-five (25) years after marriage, I am still reaping the dividends of those long time sound and godly relationships. What a joy!

Please, understand that every sound relationship requires your active participation. Therefore you must learn to constantly call on the Holy Spirit for help.

Now, in case you are into any ungodly and unprofitable relationships and you cannot see the above benefits being enjoyed by you, this is the best time to call it quit. God will not come and stop it for you. It is your responsibility to take necessary steps, right on time, before it is too late to put an end to such relationships. Stop attempting to hide behind one finger, it surely won't work!

There is so much pollution and corruption in the world today, especially in the area of relationships among singles. Refuse to be corrupted! You are the light of the world; you have nothing absolutely to do with darkness (Matthew 5:13-14). Light and darkness can never co-exist. Don't be careless in your relationships. You must get to a point where you make a covenant with God, never to involve yourself in any unhealthy relationships. Your destiny shall not be ruined!

Chapter 10

BE FINANCIALLY RESPONSIBLE!

Therefore is the kingdom of heaven likened unto a certain king, which would take account of his servants.

Matthew 18:23

Many singles feel that because they have only themselves to cater for, the subject of being financially responsible is not as crucial to them as it is for most couples. But really, nothing can be farther from the truth. Singles need more financial skills than even couples! Singles need to be financially responsible, especially because they have to face every financial challenge on their own.

Studies show that singles tend to spend more money than each member of a dual income household. Interestingly, research shows that their three top priority areas of spending are food, clothing and entertainment. These easily drain the income of singles!

This becomes very important especially in these days

of unending fashion. There are also all manner of entertainment centers, fast food and eateries springing up in every corner! Many singles do not even know how to cook anymore! There is a serious concern here! Learning some simple cooking techniques could have some dramatic positive effect on your finances. Do you know that a simple home made lunch and a bit of time out from the world, will do you a lot more good economically, psychologically and even health wise than the frantic run for fast food?

You need to be financially educated and the best time to learn the basics of money management is while you are still single. You must be able to control your day to day financial affairs. This is responsibility in action! Financial irresponsibility coupled with unholy crave for quick money, has driven many youths and singles to getting themselves involved in all manner of vices such as sexual immorality, robbery, money laundering, etc. Your financial future is dependent on how responsible you are with money handling today.

Whether you are widowed, divorced or simply single, now is the time to build and protect your financial future. Personal finance, among other things, has been proved to enhance self esteem, which is one major area of concern to many singles.

What are some of these basics of money management

that enhance financial responsibility? Let's examine some of them here.

Be Accountable

Accountability is responsibility. To be accountable is to be responsible for a thing that is done. God takes account of His creatures, He believes in giving reasons for the things that you do or spend. Jesus said every idle word shall be accounted for (Matthew. 12:36). In the Garden of Eden, God went to take account of the day and Adam was the person called to give an account of the happenings in the garden.

God will require a proper account of all the things that He had given to you including your time, gift, talent and finances. The Bible says in Romans 14:12:

So then every one of us shall give account of himself to God

You need to be accountable, not just to yourself, but primarily to God, who is the supplier of all your provisions. People around you as well as your family members should be able to see your example of accountability, so they can learn prudent spending and wise financial transactions.

Financial rest does not come when you are a millionaire. It comes by being a good money manager. You must have a financial plan or else you are creating room for financial pain. Pain is a sign of disorder, therefore to experience financial pain is a sign of disorder in your spending pattern.

Record keeping is a requirement for accountability. Have a proper documentation of your financial transactions. Learn to keep record of all your income as well as expenditure. List out your income, your expenditure and review them from time to time, so as to assess whether your financial transactions are prudent or whether you need to adjust your spending pattern.

Periodically, make a list of the items you spend money on and how much money you spend on each item. You may choose to do this monthly, weekly and or daily. Keep accurate records. There is a small dairy that I usually carry around with me where record of any money spent is kept. That way, at the end of the month, I can easily recollect whatever I spent money on during the month. With that, it becomes easy to compile a financial report. I usually submit a copy of this periodically to my husband as well. This helps me a great deal in being accountable to God who is my source, to my husband who is my head, as well as myself, so I can live in good conscience. It also enables to me set a worthy example for those around me to follow. That gives me fulfillment!

Accountability pays off. The Lord says:

...thou good and faithful servant: thou hast been faithful over a few things, I will make thee ruler over many things:

Matthew 25:21

Financial faithfulness qualifies you for financial fruitfulness. You receive more money from the Lord and from men too. More money cannot be committed into your hands, except you are accountable for the one you have at present. Financial success, just like success in any area of life, must be prepared for and one major way to do that is by being accountable.

Learn To Budget

One major thing that will help you as a single to be financially responsible is to budget for your spending. Budgeting is not a gift; rather it is an art that has to be learnt. Moreover, budgeting is Biblical! Jesus said in the book of Luke 14:28,

For which of you, intending to build a tower, sitteth not down first, and counteth the cost, whether he have sufficient to finish it

This implies that you have to sit down and reasonably plan your spending. Proper planning will give you financial rest. Planning and budgeting is necessary for proper financial management. How will you know how much you need per month, if you have not sat down to write out what your expenditure for the month is? You need to budget for both domestic needs and essential commodities. To waste what you have is an offence to the Lord. So, budgeting is very important in the life of a single.

In order to be financially responsible as a single, you need to understand what budgeting really is. A good budget is a spending plan that includes virtually everything you intend to spend money on over a specified period of time, based on the expected income. Expenditures in a wise budget include such savings as for a 'rainy day', for large purchases, giving and for future career while you still stay within your income.

Why Budgeting?

A good budgeting plan will guide your path financially. It will help you to set up guidelines for reaching your goals, which in turn enables you to measure your progress. You will then be able to control your money instead of money controlling you!

Budgeting enhances your ability to live within your means. The reason why many people are in debt and financial stress today is because they are not living within their means. If you spend beyond your means you will end up in debt. Indebtedness is disastrous! It destroys! Debt has led to the untimely death of some! You will not go to the grave before your time.

Understand that lack of contentment is the main reason many youth and singles get into debt. As singles, lean to be content with what you have per time. This enables you to live within your means. My husband says that whatever God cannot give him, may he never have it! Apostle Paul said in one of his epistles to the Philippians that:

> *Not that I speak in respect of want: for I have learned, in whatsoever state I am, therewith to be content.*
> Philippians 4:11

Learn the secret of contentment and live within your means, it makes life fulfilling and enhances your being responsible financially.

Another reason many youths and singles get into debt is covetousness. This is a strong desire for the things that other people have and wanting to have them at all cost. Remember that life does not consist in the abundance of the things you possess (Luke 12:15).

Comparison is another reason for getting into debt. Many singles compare themselves with others, forgetting they are unique before God. Don't join that kind of rat race. There is no wisdom in comparing yourself with others (2 Corinthians 10:12).

A budget is a financial guide that helps you measure your progress in a bid, to realizing your financial goals and dreams. Living without a budget is like living without a guide, it makes life miserable and frustrating. It limits your financial greatness! Can you imagine the Government or a major corporation operating without a budget? No and neither should you. You cannot be single with a difference without adherence to these financial principles.

Prioritize Your Spending

To prioritize is to put things in order of importance, so that you can deal with the most important ones first. You can prioritize your spending and maximize your income. Spend within your means and be content with your income size per time. The Bible gives us a great word of comfort: *"though thy beginning be small, yet thy latter end should greatly increase"* (Job 8:7). Learn contentment. It is the gateway to great gains (1 Timothy 6:6).

In handling money, learn to write down your needs and then draw a scale of preference. The fact is, you can never exhaust your needs but there are those that must come before others. These are your priorities. You must make sure that you do not spend money on things that you can afford to leave till a latter date. Ascertain the things that you need in order of importance and buy them accordingly. This is priority spending!

Do not spend money carelessly. Spend money on what

is expedient, not just what is lawful. The scripture says:

All things are lawful unto me, but all things are not expedient: all things are lawful for me, but I will not be brought under the power of any.

1 Corinthians 6:12

Don't just spend money as the need arises, else you may find out that you have spent all your earnings on areas of less importance, while the most important areas are left unattended to. Of course, not all expenditure is right. Prioritizing enables you to distinguish between right and wrong expenditure.

Stay clear of indebtedness for God hates it. How do you know God hates indebtedness? You may ask. The Bible says:

Owe no man anything ...

Romans 1:8

Whatever God hates, you should hate, this is godliness in action. It is godly to flee indebtedness. There are certain things you buy on credit that could wait till a later date. What do you gain buying clothes, shoes, jewelry, television set, telephone handset, etc. on credit when the ones you have are not complaining? Who are you trying to impress? Please, live your size per time and cut off from friends who drive you to live above your means. Engage in buying things that are necessary and vital per time for God hates waste (John 6:12).

Financial discipline is one major benefit of prioritized spending. You train yourself to put your spending pattern under control. The best time to practise this is while you are still single. It then becomes a way of life before you get into marriage. This in turn makes for financial rest and fruitfulness, which many singles lack today.

Prudence is another benefit of priority spending. This enables you to make sensible and careful financial decisions, thereby avoiding unnecessary risks. I believe this is why the bible says:

> *...the prudent man looketh well to his going.*
>
> Proverbs 14: 15b

And

> *A prudent man foreseeth the evil, and hideth himself: but the simple pass on, and are punished.*
>
> Proverbs 22: 3; 27: 12

That the above scripture is repeated verbatim in two separate places is not a coincidence! You cannot be prudent and not be financially responsible.

Also, priority spending frees you from financial waste. Many youths and singles regret after spending money on certain things, simply because they have not prioritized their expenditure. This amounts to a waste. Remember that God hates waste! To waste money is to waste means. Whatever you waste, you will eventually lack. If you waste money, you will surely lack it! A waster will surely end up in want. The story of the prodigal son in the scriptures paints this picture very clearly.

> *And not many days after the younger son gathered all together, and took his journey into a far country, and there wasted his substance with riotous living.*
>
> *And when he had spent all, there arose a mighty famine in that land; and he began to be in want.*
>
> Luke 15: 13-14

However, the good news is that you cannot engage in priority spending and be a waster at the same time. Learn to order your priorities right. Mix prudence with contentment and enjoy great gain (1 Timothy 6:6).

Shun idleness

> *... but he that gathereth by labour shall increase.*
>
> Proverbs 13:11

Your financial relevance and increase has a lot to do with your ability to engage in profitable ventures. Work to earn money! Refuse to be idle. Let your hands be working hands. God is a God of multiplication. But if you earn nothing, what will He multiply? Zero multiplied a thousand times over, still equals zero! To make a difference financially as a single, you must work diligently.

There are many young people who are lazy and idle

today. They like to have and spend money but do not want to work for it. They want 'cheap' money. They fail to remember that 'cheap' money cheapen destiny! Such people need to realize that only money earned through the right channel is sweet to spend.

Be sure you are gainfully employed. If you cannot find the kind of employment you really want, make sure you find something to do while you search for what you really want. Avoid and discourage idleness by all means. This is why the Bible says:

Whatsoever thy hand findeth to do, do it with thy might;
Ecclesiastes 9: 10

There is dignity in labour! It is work that enhances your worth. Not to work is to loose worth. The purpose of your working is not just for your personal upkeep, but it will help you to be a blessing to others. In blessing others you also stand in the position of being blessed.

Do not rely on the gifts from your Uncle, Aunty, parents, Christian brothers and sisters. Remember the command in God's word:

For even when we were with you, this we commanded you, that if any would not work, neither should he eat.
2 Thesselonians 3: 10

Investments and savings

Many singles today, find it difficult to save part of their

203

earnings. Many are ignorant of what it means to invest. If you have a good understanding of the profit that is in savings and investment, you will key yourself into it.

The idea of saving and investment is not a worldly principle, it is very scriptural. Even the Lord Jesus had a treasurer (John 13: 29), who kept some amount in case of need. In one of the parables of Jesus, the reason why the man was further punished by his master was because he did not invest his money neither did he work with it. He told him:

> *Thou oughtest therefore to have put my money to the exchangers, and then at my coming I should have received mine own with usury.*
>
> Matthew 25:27

This simple illustration shows that it is very profitable to invest.

Joseph, on the other hand saved the entire land of Egypt from famine by engaging the principle of saving. A percentage of their annual harvest was kept in the store against the days of scarcity.

> *And in the seven plenteous years the earth brought forth by handfuls.*
>
> *And he gathered up all the food of the seven years, which were in the land of Egypt, and laid up the food in the cities: the food of the field,, which was*

round about every city, laid he up in the same.

And the seven years of dearth began to come, according as Joseph had said: and the dearth was in all lands; but in all the land of Egypt there was bread.

And all countries came into Egypt to Joseph for to buy corn; ...

Genesis 41: 47,48,54,57.

The truth is there is seed in every income that gets into your hand. Do not eat your seed with your harvest like many people do. If you eat your seed today you will beg tomorrow. Your seed is to be sown and the first and sure place to put your treasure is in the kingdom of God. Your primary investment is your tithe, which is the preservative for other forms of investments. There are other kingdom investments, but in all, you must be sure that God is your priority.

Spending money foolishly is one major cause of borrowing and lack. To avoid such, investments should be engaged in. Set aside some amount on a regular basis and invest it. How big the amount is, is not as important as the regularity and consistency. Also, diversify by including many types of investments. This saves you the embarrassment of borrowing, especially in times of need. Benjamin Franklin said "He that goes a borrowing goes a sorrowing". Don't bring sorrow into your life through borrowing!

Covenant practice

To be distinguished financially, you have a responsibility to walk in the covenant. The quality of your covenant walk with God determines how financially buoyant you will ever be. You cannot walk in the covenant and end up small financially. The word says:

> *If they obey and serve him, they shall spend their days in prosperity, and their years in pleasures.*
>
> Job 36:11

When you obey God and walk in the covenant, prosperity and financial pleasure answers to you. As a covenant practitioner, tithing is primary. Tithe is the 10% of your income, profit or gifts received. According to God's word:

> *And all the tithe of the land, whether of the seed of the land, or of the fruit of the tree, is the Lord's: it is holy unto the LORD.*
>
> Leviticus 27:30

To fail to pay your tithe is to rob God! Just think for a moment. Is it possible to rob God and not be caught? But when you do not pay your tithe that is what you are doing! Don't rob God in your attempt to save money or make up for some unforeseen expenses.

Your tithe is an acknowledgement and recognition that God is the source of all the money that comes to you in the first place. Your tithe is also your spiritual insurance of all your income against all devourers. To refuse to pay tithe opens you up to devourers.

The Lord says, when you pay tithes,

... I will rebuke the devourer for your sakes, and he shall not destroy the fruits of your ground ...
Malachi 3:11

This covenant practice is an insurance against devourers like sickness, accident, business failure etc which are devices of Satan to rob you of financial progress. Your tithes are to be paid in bulk to the Lord in the church, where you are being spiritually fed; not to a man, not to the poor or an organization. Tithes are for the Lord. He alone gives instructions on how it would be utilized.

If you find it difficult to pay tithe while you are still single, how will you survive when you get into marriage? If you cannot tithe now that you earn a meager salary, how would you make it when your income is bigger? If it is difficult for you to tithe out of what is given you, now that you are still a student, what will happen when you start working to earn money yourself?

Your tithe is to be given willingly and cheerfully for it to be acceptable unto God! Since when I was single, I have always paid my tithe promptly, willingly, excitedly and rejoicing. This has in no small way made it very easy for me, up till now, over twenty-five (25) years after marriage to do the same! Truly, giving is living!

Apart from tithing, other forms of covenant practice include giving of offerings whenever you attend service. This is to be done according to how God has blessed you. The word of God says you should not appear before Him empty handed (Exodus 23:15; 34:20).

Others include Prophet Offerings, giving to kingdom projects, giving to your parents and relations, giving to the needy, etc. Do these according to your financial level per time. It is not the volume that actually matters, but the obedience. You can maximize your finance by totally giving yourself to this covenant practice. Be consistent and diligent in it and before you know it, you shall be financially distinguished.

Things To Avoid

To manage money responsibly, there are certain things that you must avoid. Let us briefly examine some of them here.

Covetousness

And he said unto them, Take heed, and beware of covetousness: for a man's life consisteth not in the abundance of the things which he possesseth.

Luke 12:15

Covetousness is the desire for things that do not belong to you. It is the craving to get those things by all means. It is the excessive desire and greed for gain. This is a major challenge to the financial future of many today. This is an indication of lack of integrity.

Covetousness subtly takes hold of many singles these days because of peer pressure. Every one is out to get the latest item in the market. This crave make many singles spend beyond their means. This has pushed many into debt and all manner of unbelievable vices. Many have developed affection for money rather than for God. Money has taken the place of God in many hearts today. This is abomination and God hates it!

You cannot serve God and money. The Bible says:

No man can serve two masters: for either he will hate the one, and love the other; or else he will hold to the one, and despise the other; Ye cannot serve God and mammon.

Matthew 6:24

Money seeks to be worshipped and served, but if you serve money you will mourn. Only God is worthy to be worshipped, not money.

In his days, the man Job was the greatest in the East. Yet, he did not get his wealth through crookedness!

The Bible records that he was perfect and upright; feared God and eschewed evil. He was a man full of integrity (Job 1:1). So, you can have financial integrity in this crooked world. If Job could, then you can.

Gehazi on the other hand, could not understand why Elisha his master 'spared' Naaman, after he was healedof his leprosy. So, Gehazi out of covetousness ran after Naaman and forcefully collected gifts from him. He ended up collecting Naaman's leprosy also (2 Kings 5:20-27). What a disaster! He would have succeeded Elisha if he had not been covetous. A glorious future awaits you; don't sell off to covetousness.

Many young people have lost their jobs, positions, promotions and good recommendations from others due to their greed and excessive desire for ungodly gains. So, they go through life struggling without making a way! You can not afford to lose your destiny to money. Life is more important than money! Do not corner what does not belong to you. Covetousness is idolatry, but you can be free from it and enjoy financial freedom.

The cure for covetousness is contentment. Apostle Paul said:

But godliness with contentment is great gain.

And having food and raiment let us be therewith content.
1 Timothy 6:6, 8

Be satisfied with the step by step lifting of God in

your life. Patience is required. Just as a child does not walk the day it is born, you should not expect to become a millionaire overnight. Covetousness will destroy your financial progress and future. So you need to walk in total contentment and godly wisdom to sustain your wealth.

Life is in phases and men are in sizes. Live your size, eat your size and wear your size per time. Running after clothes, possessions, money, cars etc, more than necessary, at the expenses of your fellowship with God, will put you in deep financial troubles. Don't be attached to possession (Psalms 62:10), but rather set your affection on things above and guard your heart against the deceit of riches (Colossians 3:1-3, Luke 8:14).

Impulsive spending

This is buying things suddenly without stopping to think carefully about what might happen as a result of such action. Such purchases could make you exceed your budget. Because you have money in your pocket, does not mean you must spend it on unbudgeted items. Beware of impulsive spending and don't just buy something because you have money; Buy things because they are necessary. Be disciplined to follow your budget strictly.

Impulsive buyers buy on a whim. They make unplanned purchases and usually lack self-control in buying situations. They lack clear priorities in spending.

This results in overspending, unnecessary additional debt, unused articles that will end up as wastes. Most impulsive spenders sabotage their own prosperity with the "I want it now syndrome," which is characterized by spending beyond their incomes.

Discipline is the key to controlling impulsive buying. Do not let this habit overcome you. Remember,

> ... *for of whom a man is overcome, of the same is he brought in bondage.*
>
> 2 Peter 2:19

To overcome impulsive spending, do the following:

Pray: The Bible says, commit your ways unto the Lord and he will direct thy path. I have come to discover that nothing is too small to pray for and commit unto God. Put all spending under God's control. With God's guidance, you will be able to spend on things that will give you peace at the end of the day.

Also, discipline will help put your spending under control. Once spending has been brought under control, determine how much needs to be spent each month and stick to the budget.

Be accountable to someone for a period of time. It could be to either your parents or somebody that you can trust. You can also establish a "want-to-buy" list. Then wait seven days and find two additional prices for the same item. If there is still a need or want for the item after a week, go ahead and buy it. Nevertheless, only one item can be on the "want-to-buy" list at a time.

Avoiding impulse spending doesn't mean that you can never buy what you want. It just means saving up your earnings to enable you pay cash and in the end have fulfillment.

Lack of accountability

To be accountable is to be responsible for your financial decisions and be able to give a satisfactory reason for your actions. This calls for faithfulness, among other things. The Word says:

> *He that is faithful in that which is least is faithful also in much: and he that is unjust in the least is unjust also in much.*

Luke 16: 10

Financial faithfulness does not happen suddenly neither is it an over-night issue. Rather, it comes by constant practice and discipline. If you can't develop discipline, accountability, faithfulness, planning and budgeting skill when your income is N5,000 (five Thousand Naira), there is no guarantee that you will not lose control when it becomes N500, 000 (Five Hundred Thousand Naira).

If in your single days you are neck deep in debt, what

will happen when you are married? God is pleased with those that can effectively account for the things entrusted into their hands.

> *If therefore ye have not been faithful in the unrighteous mammon, who will commit to your trust the true riches?*
>
> Luke 16:11

Comparison

You must avoid comparison, to be a good manager of money. Many young people suffer from peer pressure, comparing themselves with their mates and thereby losing financial integrity (2 Corinthians 10:12). Remember that you are not like any other, so also your destiny is unique. Don't be deceived by what others get themselves involved in. You have your own life to live and you are solely responsible for it.

Idleness and Borrowing

Idleness can bury a man's destiny just as borrowing can turn one to a servant (Ecclesiastes 10:18; Proverbs 22:7). You must avoid them, if you desire to live a financially responsible life. By the grace of God, I can boldly say anywhere that I have never borrowed!

Right now, I curse every spirit of idleness, borrowing, ungodly comparison and everything targeted at destroying your financial future in Jesus' name. I decree your liberty right now. Be loosed never to be entangled again in Jesus name. Amen!

Congratulations and welcome to your season of financial positive turnaround!

Chapter 11

MIND YOUR CARRIAGE AND COMPORTMENT

Now then we are ambassadors for Christ, as though God did beseech you by us: ...

2 Corinthians 2: 20

One fundamental issue that runs through the lives of many singles is the lack of a proper understanding of their worth or importance. This explains why many young people look to the wrong sources for acceptance, help, comfort or counsel. Some even choose the wrong profession, all in an attempt to cover up. Others get involved in all manner of vices such as occultism, drugs, wrong relationships and the like, seeking from external sources something which is actually locked within them. To a large extent, the way you carry and comport yourself affects your worth and acceptance.

Do you know that the way you walk says a lot about your person? Those slumped shoulders and dragging feet are reflective of your mood! If you are insecure for example, you will walk provocatively. Are you moody, feeling heavy and frustrated? Begin to take note; you will discover how much this reflects in your carriage and comportment.

To enhance your worth and importance therefore, you must learn how to carry and comport yourself appropriately. Restructure your walk to match and reflect God's description of you as His ambassador. Learn to walk tall! Walk straight! Walk smartly, not sluggishly! When you walk from henceforth, lift up your head and straighten your shoulders! Walk with honor and dignity. As you do, you will be maximizing the grace of God upon your life: distinguishing yourself as a single. I guarantee you, this will automatically affect your worth and acceptance! This will also be a rich investment into your future life; the dividend that you will keep drawing from as long as you live, as it is in mine!

What Is Carriage and Comportment?

The word 'carriage' means the way in which somebody holds and moves the head and body. So, your carriage is the characteristic way of bearing your body. 'Comportment' means posture, stance, and movement. It means the way to bear, conduct, bring together, carry and to behave in a manner conformable to what is proper and expected.

One of the most important questions you must ask yourself is "How am I conducting myself?" If your life is to attract, influence people and impact on them as designed, then you must begin to conduct yourself in a manner that reflects that expectation.

In order to conduct yourself in a manner that reflects your expectation, you must be sure of the value you carry. For anything to reflect on the outside it must take root from within; for the abundance of what is within is what overflows out.

In this chapter, we shall be exploring the secrets of how to carry and comport yourself with elegance, without any pretence or ingenuity. This understanding will surely bring you added value, meaning, joy, fulfillment; which will enhance your worth and acceptance, bringing you fulfillment in life. Follow very closely here as we examine these secrets.

A Discovery of Your Life Purpose

This is the first secret. There's something that you were uniquely created for to accomplish on this earth. Jeremiah 1:5 says:

> *Before I formed thee in the belly I knew thee; and before thou camest forth out of the womb I sanctified thee, and I ordained thee a prophet unto the nations.*

So, there is something that you and only you, can

do. That is what you are fashioned for in your generation. But you have a responsibility to discover it; to find it out. This explains why the Bible says:

It is the glory of God to conceal a thing: but the honour of kings is to search out a matter.

Proverbs 25:2

Discovery is the art of finding out, what already exists but is not yet known. When you discover your life purpose, it will influence every other aspect of your life. You will have the key to happiness, satisfaction and fulfillment. Your carriage and comportment can be most significantly enhanced, when you are doing something that you are shaped for. You can only fulfill your innermost aspirations when you engage in doing something that interests you, which holds your attention; something you are created for. May you find it on time!

Accept and Believe in What God made You to be

Here is the second secret. You didn't just happen, you were made! You are also not an after thought, you were specially crafted! The Bible says:

Know ye that the LORD he is God: it is he that hath made us, and not we ourselves; we are his people, and the sheep of his pasture.

Psalms 100:3

It is crucial for you to accept and believe in what God has made you to be. What has God made you to be? An understanding of this will definitely enhance your carriage and comportment in no small measure.

A new creature: At salvation, you became a new creature (2 Corinthians 5:17). Your lineage changed for the better. You became a member of God's family, where Jesus belongs. Old things such as sin, guilt, condemnation, are passed away; you are now brand new! Not a modification of your old status, but totally brand new. Congratulations! You now have what it takes to walk in the newness of life.

A royal priesthood: You belong to royalty (1 Peter 2:9). You are a royal being - a king, queen, prince, princess. In the natural, these have their way of carrying themselves with elegance; they live in the consciousness of who they are and where they come from. This affects how they present themselves. Even in the public, their comportment is unique. Spiritually, this is who God has made you. So, learn a lesson from the natural. Carry yourself with royalty from henceforth, comport yourself as a king and queen. You are unique!

Salt of the earth: Salt sweetens and preserves, among other things. It has a very pleasant, special and enjoyable taste and flavour when applied. It adds value. This is who you are on this earth, to give it taste (Matthew 5:13).

This is meant to reflect in the way you carry and comport yourself. May you not lose your savour!

The light of the world (Matthew 5:13-16). Light makes it possible to see things, thereby avoiding stumbling. As light to your world, you are meant to illuminate your generation, set the pace by taking the lead in showing others how to get things done. You are also meant to give direction to your world. So, when darkness covers the earth and gross darkness the people, you lighten it; demonstrating it among other things by the way you carry and comport yourself. Your light shall never be turned to darkness.

You are an ambassador (2 Corinthians 5:20). You are a representative of Jesus on earth, so, you are by privilege, to enjoy the immunity of heaven. This gives you authority against everything contrary to your wellbeing here on earth, in every area of your life, such as your health, mind, future etc. This in turn should affect the way you carry yourself! You are what God says you are! Now that you are still single, believe it, think it, behave it and it will naturally affect your carriage and comportment.

Live Life One Day at a Time

Thirdly, it is important that you learn to live your life one day at a time. Many young people today are anxious about life and this deals a deadly blow on them, eventually affecting the way they carry and comport themselves. The Bible says:

> *Be anxious for nothing, but in everything by prayer and supplication with thanksgiving, let your request be made known to God.*
>
> Philippians 4:6 (NAS)

Surely, anxiety-causing situations will arise, but the good news is that what it takes to overcome is within reach. We live in a world filled with negativism, misfortune, chaos, calamity, disaster, pressure, stress and the list is endless! Hardly does any newspaper report bring joy. Jesus lived an anxiety-free life, so you can too.

In many young people, anxiety has led to fear - of tomorrow, failure, rejection and so on. In others, it has led to the hurry to 'make it' in life, which in turn lures them to getting involved in many unbelievable vices. They cannot wait for their tomorrow, they want to live it today. As far as some are concerned, God is too slow for them in this fast world! Some others are plagued with peer pressure, which leads to covetousness and the like.

Do not forget that every big thing in life starts small. Every tree with fruits came out of a seed. Every long journey begins with one little step after another and with time eventually gets accomplished! Remember the popular saying, Rome was not built in a day? The same is true about life! God is not slow (2 Peter 3: 9).

The cares, riches and pleasures of this life choke up the destinies of many youths and singles thereby robbing them of the exemplary lifestyle they are destined to live (Luke 8:14). But as for you, your case is different. So, when men say there is a casting down you keep saying there is a lifting up.

The truth is, anxiety is not a friend but an enemy! It is not from God but from the devil. Its mission? To steal your joy, kill your peace; destroy your confidence in God. It makes your relationship with God sour and in the ultimate destroys destiny. All of these have a way of terribly affecting the way you carry and comport yourself. It is a thief and must be caught!

But how do I catch this 'thief'? You may ask.

First, agree that you can catch it and deal with it. Second, learn to be grateful both to God and to man; refusing either murmuring or complaining irrespective of the situation you find yourself in life. Then, learn to talk to God about every area of concern in your life. And of course, build up your confidence in God through His word. This will help you to appropriately carry and comport yourself correctly. You should also live each day of your life as it comes to the full. You shall not fail!

Guard Your Thoughts

If there is any aspect of your life that you need to

guard jealously, it is your thoughts. This is the fourth secret to be examined here. Your thinking defines your living! The entirety of your life is your thoughts made flesh. You need to free yourself from the mire of lack of vigour to forge ahead in life. Be aware that success as well as failure, starts in the mind. It is not an outside event, but a product of your thoughts.

When you change your thoughts, your feelings change; when your feelings change, your behaviour changes. This change produces a change in your experience. When your experiences change, your beliefs, attitude and perspective to life also change. When your beliefs and attitude change, **YOU** change. It all begins from your thought. So, think straight!

The Bible says:

For as he thinketh in his heart, so is he:

Proverbs 23:7

Your thoughts form the basis of your speech. It affects the way you behave, determines your motives for dressing, the way you act and sets the pace for how you walk. Your comportment is determined to a large extent by your thought pattern. It therefore becomes important for you to manage your thoughts effectively.

In order to properly manage and guard the thoughts of your heart, these three things require your consideration:

Study the Word - The place of the word of God in your thought life cannot be over-emphasized. As singles, it is true that you have a busy schedule, but time spent studying the word is time invested. There is an adage in the computer world: garbage in, garbage out. It is only the word that you have fed into your spirit that overflows to affect the way you comport yourself on the outside.

Read and study the Bible. Listen to anointed messages and teachings – audio and video. As long as you keep feeding the word of God into your heart, it will govern your thoughts, determine your way of life and ultimately affect your destiny (Colossians 3:16). If you begin to think healthy thoughts, you will live a healthy life.

Philippians 4:8 outlines what you must think about

Finally, brethren, whatsoever things are true, whatsoever things are honest, whatsoever things are just, whatsoever things are pure, whatsoever things are lovely, whatsoever things are of good report; if there be any virtue, and if there be any praise, think on these things.

When you discipline yourself to think only what the Word of God permits, your thoughts will be pleasing to God and you know, those who please God, don't depreciate but appreciate!

Meditate on the Word - Meditation is the art of pondering on what you are studying, until it begins to make sense to you. Think deeply on the word, until you practically know what to do to go forward. The word of God is designed to profit you, but it cannot do so until you give it the desired attention. The Bible says:

> *All scripture is given by the inspiration of God, and is profitable...*
>
> 2 Timothy 3: 16.

But for it to profit you as a person, 1 Timothy 4:15 says:

> *Meditate upon these things; give thyself wholly to them; that thy profiting may appear to all.*

Interestingly, no one can meditate for you. Meditation is a personal, non-transferable responsibility. It has to be a deliberate act, it does not happen accidentally. Accept responsibility for qualitative, calculated meditation on God's word. Would you? If you do, without a doubt, your profiting will certainly appear to all, reflecting in your carriage and comportment.

Guard your mind - Your mind is yours; what goes on in it, is what you allow. Definitely, the devil will bring negative thoughts into your mind, but you either allow it or rebuke it. In other words, you are the architect of your own destiny; the sooner you accept responsibility, the better for you. Don't say, "I don't have a choice." You do! Remember that you make your choice and your choice makes you! Choose positive destiny-moulding thoughts, over ordinary sinful thoughts and you are on your way up. I see you get there (Proverbs 4: 23).

Be Joyful!

Joy is the fifth secret that we are examining here. Talking about the essence of joy, the Bible says:

> *The vine is dried up, and the fig tree languisheth;*
> *the pomegranate tree, the palm tree also, and the*
> *apple tree, even all the trees of the field, are withered:*
> *because joy is withered away from the sons of men.*
>
> Joel 1:12

Everything dries up when joy is missing. But, when you are joyful, you bounce around as if there is a spring underneath your feet. A merry heart provokes an attitude that makes you irresistible. It evidently affects your carriage. You cannot be joyful without reflecting it in your comportment.

The Bible says:

> *Again I will build thee, and thou shalt be built, O*
> *virgin of Israel: thou shalt again be adorned with*
> *thy tabrets, and shalt go forth in the dances of them*
> *that make merry.*
>
> Jeremiah 31:4

Joy in your heart, has a way of causing you to blossom and bloom. It refreshes you and makes you attractive. You are ever full of smiles. Your shoulders are never allowed to hang down. The joy of the Lord on your inside becomes infectious. People just want to be around you, because there is an assurance that all their own sorrows will be drowned by the joy you carry. Your youth is renewed.

With joy, you look younger than your age, your vitality is in top gear and your approach to life makes you carry yourself in a manner that is attractive. That is the secret to remaining attractive.

Don't ever allow your moods to determine how you walk; rather, let your discovery in God's word do. Be joyful and maintain it. As far as God is concerned, no matter the situation, you are a creature of great value. God is mindful of you, so walk tall! Lift up your head and straighten your shoulders! Let your walk reflect strength, health, honour, dignity and a sense of purpose. As you do, you are surely going to make a difference!

Maintaining Joy: How do I maintain joy? You may ask. The following guidelines will surely be of a tremendous help.

Firstly, you can maintain joy by a life of total gratitude to God. Be grateful to God, in and for all things. Understand that He cannot mismanage your life; He is working everything together for your good. Be grateful to God daily. Avoid complaining and murmuring (I Corinthians 10:10). It drains your joyful disposition.

Furthermore, **keep company with joyful people;** don't waste your time by hanging out with negative people. This is because joy is contagious! Remember, birds of a feather, flock together! Stick with a circle of enthusiastic and optimistic friends. This will help you maintain joy.

In addition, **fight depression** because it dries the bones. It ultimately affects your comportment and gives a negative impression about your person.

It is only with joy that you can release the great deposits within you for the Bible says:

> *Therefore with joy shall ye draw water out of the wells of salvation.*
>
> Isaiah 12:3

Joy is a fruit of the Spirit and the Holy Spirit is given in measures to those, who have received Jesus Christ as their Lord and personal Saviour. Outside of the Holy Spirit, what you have is happiness and that is determined only by the happenings around you. That is why, happiness does not last. It is centered on an event and as soon as that event disappears, so also does the happiness disappear. But with joy, the Bible says:

> *He that believeth on me, as the scripture hath said,*

out of his belly shall flow rivers of living water.
                                                John 7:38.

It is a continuous flow that cannot be stopped. Now, in Jesus name, I come against every thing that saps you and drains your joy, I curse it and release the flow of joy into your life henceforth. Receive it in Jesus name! Amen.

Other things that will enhance your carriage and comportment, making you live a positively different life as a single include the following:

Speak right

This is another secret that has to be examined. It is important for you to know that the words of your mouth, influence your carriage. God respects what flows out of your mouth because it is your God-given creative tool. That is why the Bible says:

> *Death and life are in the power of the tongue: and they that love it shall eat the fruit thereof.*
> Proverbs 18: 21

The word 'fruit' stands for outcome, reward, consequence, effect, etc. That means, whatever your outcome, look closely, your tongue is responsible for it!

You cannot keep speaking death and expect to reap life, it is not possible. If you want a transformed life, speak right words, because the force for transformation lies in right words (Job 6:25). Do you know that even your salvation is tied to the words of your mouth? Your healing and health is also tied to the words of your mouth (Proverbs 16:14).

The Bible in Job 6:25 says:

How forcible are right words!

They carry heavenly forces to deliver man's desires. It begins by finding the right words. Your world is actually framed by your words. Whatever your desires, give it expression by speaking it out! Think before you speak and speak only what you want. Don't speak carelessly. No wonder, therefore, that God declares that He will hold us accountable for every word we speak.

But I say unto you, That every idle word that men shall speak, they shall give account thereof in the day of judgment.

For by thy words thou shalt be justified, and by thy words thou shalt be condemned.

Matthew 12:36-37

It is high time you learn how to speak in line with the word of God. The angels of God are at an alert ready to execute your words. They do not have respect for your words spoken in 'error' (Ecclesiastes 5:6).

God's Word in Numbers 14:28 says:

... As truly as I live, saith the LORD, as ye have spoken in mine ears, so will I do to you.

God is committed to whatsoever He hears you say, whether you mean it or not.

Your words must reflect the dignity of Christ that you represent. Let your words be seasoned with grace that they may minister grace to every hearer. Your speech should be such that commands attention. Your words tell a lot about your person.

However, it is from the abundance of your heart that your mouth speaks. If your heart is loaded with the right stuff, you will speak right. Concerning Sarah, the Bible says:

Even as Sara obeyed Abraham, calling him lord: whose daughters ye are, as long as ye do well, and are not afraid with any amazement.

1 Peter 3:6

Sarah had so much respect for her husband. She rated him so highly, that what she called him was important to her. Her respect for him, found expression in her speech by the name she called him.

The same way, if you are loaded with junk, one word from your lips and everyone around you, will be able to tell the level of filthiness within. Jesus said:

O generation of vipers, how can ye, being evil, speak

232

good things? for out of the abundance of the heart the mouth speaketh.

A good man out of the good treasure of the heart bringeth forth good things: and an evil man out of the evil treasure bringeth forth evil things.

Matthew 12:34-35.

Watch what goes on inside of you!

Then, don't be hasty in speech; watch how much you speak. The Bible says:

In the multitude of words there wanteth not sin: but he that refraineth his lips is wise.

Proverbs 10:19

Someone for instance, who does not know when to keep quiet is a natural nuisance to everyone around. You must learn when to refrain from speaking, even if you are a naturally outspoken person.

Behave Right!

Your behaviour is the seventh secret to a life of proper carriage and packaging. Your behaviour is so important to your destiny that it determines how far you go in life. God weighs your behaviour and uses it to determine your placement. The Bible says:

... for the LORD is a God of knowledge, and by him actions are weighed.

1 Samuel 2: 3.

The word 'behaviour' means, "the manner of conducting oneself; it is the mode in which one bears or comports oneself. It also means act, work, function or reactions in a particular way." As a Christian, your actions are important because you are a pacesetter and a creature of envy. Wherever you may be schooling or working, see yourself as God's representative there and accept the responsibility to act as an ambassador of Christ.

If you want to be truly great, you must accept the responsibility to behave right. Each time you want to react in a particular way, ask yourself, "What will the consequence of my reaction be?"

As a single person with a mission, constantly examine your behaviour. No one wants to have a terror around, not even as a neighbour nor as a co-worker. So, to constantly quarrel, nag or even fight around could be a deterrent to the people around you.

Interestingly, the thing about behaviour is this: more people are watching you than you are conscious of. One minute of unbridled anger can erase twenty years of good report. When you fight at the bus stop, for instance, people are watching you and you will be amazed at how many people can recognise you later in life from that singular incidence. You cannot afford that kind of carelessness.

One of my daughters in Christ had this testimony.

When her spouse first met her, he found out that she had attended the same university with his cousin, who of course, she did not know intimately. So, he decided to ask his cousin questions about this sister. One interesting thing the cousin said was that: getting married to her would be a great asset. Not because she had possessions, but that her life was a very positive testimony in her university days. She happened to be one of those girls that were well spoken of by most people on campus.

The Bible says:

> *Ye are the light of the world. A city that is set on an hill cannot be hid.*
>
> Matthew 5:14

You carry a light that attracts and like a city that is on a hill, you cannot be hidden. You may even wonder how people see you. But, that is the word of God in action. You have no hiding place for misbehaviour. Therefore, consciously caution yourself to be of good behaviour at all times.

No one was born rowdy. So, don't say to your self: 'that is my nature.' Every child is born blank. Whatever you exhibit is what has been fed into you somehow, either by your parents, your environment, the society, the books you read or the people you associate with. You can therefore decide one day, to make a positive change.

How then should you act? The Bible says:

> *I therefore, the prisoner for the Lord, appeal to you to walk (lead a life) worthy of the (divine) calling to which you have been called (with behaviour) that is a credit to the summons to God's service.*
>
> *(Living as becomes you) with complete lowliness of mind (humility) and meekness (unselfishness, gentleness, mildness). With patience, bearing with one another and making allowances because you love one another.*
>
> Ephesians 4: 1-2(Amplified)

God expects you to behave your calling! Let qualities like meekness, patience, gentleness and unselfishness be obvious in your life. Cultivate them.

Paul speaking about the gifts of the Spirit said,

> *But covet earnestly the best gifts:*
>
> **1 Corinthians 12:31**

The fruit of the Spirit can be coveted and acquired. Gentleness is of great value and it can be made available to as many as will seek it.

Be Confident

Finally, another secret is that you need to develop an unshakable level of confidence that makes you virtually unstoppable. You can set very clear, challenging and yet, realistic goals and then make plans to accomplish them. You should be taking them step-by-step, each day, in the direction of your dominant aspirations. Believe in yourself, do not be intimidated by your setbacks because God never makes mistakes. Build up on your strengths to make up for your weakness.

Dress Sense

This chapter on carriage and comportment cannot be concluded without reference to your dress sense, because your dressing reflects your values, self worth, taste, etc. The way you dress is the way you will be addressed.

In the beginning, God clothed the first man and woman.

> *Unto Adam also and to his wife did the LORD God make coats of skins, and clothed them.*
>
> Genesis 3:21

So, the primary purpose of dressing is to cover man's nakedness in a way to please his Creator. Other reasons are: To be elegant and dynamic in our day-to-day activities; to serve as a role model to both the saved and unsaved; to protect from heat, cold, physical injuries, etc.

Clothing has been an important form of expression; giving meaning to our ethnicity, social status, personal identity, generation and of course style and fashion.

Even though you are created a free moral person, with the capacity to make decisions, you have to make use of your creative mind to filter your dressing to glorify God primarily. Your dressing should make you and everyone that sees you 'comfortable' (1 Corinthians 6:12). You should ask yourself, what does my dress tell others about me? Does it draw attention to the 'me' or bring glory to God?

1 Timothy 2:9-10 admonishes

In like manner also, that women adorn themselves in modest apparel, with shamefacedness and sobriety; not with broided hair, or gold, or pearls, or costly array;

But (which becometh women professing godliness) with good works.

'Modest' is being orderly, well-arranged. In other words, clothing that is neat and appropriate for the occasion. *The Webster's College Dictionary* defines modest as: "having or showing regard for the decencies of behaviour, speech, dress, etc.; decent."

'Shamefacedness,' means to dress with the sense of decency or respectability. 'Sobriety' is being sound minded, self controlled, of good judgment and moderate.

As singles who are determined to make a difference, even your dressing should reflect your mission. Be modest, decent and moderate. Your dressing does not have to reveal the sensitive parts of your body else, it is an abuse.

Ladies, if you are 'swimming' around other men and women, respect them. Honestly, they do not benefit in the least from being knocked out dead by your sensuality. Why provoke jealousy or be a stumbling block? It's not scriptural.

This is where 'being our best' has a fine line. Some may very well 'appreciate' it, but it is not appropriate. Find decent clothes to wear as a respect for your role and goals in life. Be aware, if you are bare, *realize how carefully you are going to need to carry yourself a*nd realize how you will be perceived. Be comfortable and confident in what you wear. But, protect your feminine "power". It is a gift. The same goes for the young men.

Dress to win souls, not to weaken them. Your dressing reveals who you are and what you are up to and that is exactly the response you will receive. You are the light of the world, so let that light shine in you so your Father in heaven will be glorified.

In conclusion, take personal responsibility over your life. Pay attention to how you carry yourself and you will surely be positively different. How you comport yourself will determine how far you go in the race of life. Your packaging will always affect your product; so refuse to live your life carelessly! You will surely make it!

Chapter 12

OVERCOMING LONELINESS

I looked on my right hand, and beheld, but there was no man that would know me: refuge failed me; no man cared for my soul.

I cried unto thee, O LORD: I said, Thou art my refuge and my portion in the land of the living.

Psalms 142:4-5

One of the common plagues among youths and singles, which is responsible for why many rush into relationships, most of which end up in regret, is loneliness. In an attempt to alleviate this plague, some have been pressured into taking decisions that have ruined their destinies.

Everyone, including myself, at one time or another has had to deal with loneliness. But the good news is, you can overcome it rather than it overcoming you! So, the earlier you learn how to overcome it the better.

Let me state clearly here from the outset that loneliness is completely different from being alone. You could be alone without being lonely.

Loneliness is the awareness that you lack meaningful contact with others. It involves a feeling of inner emptiness which can be accompanied by discouragement, sadness, a sense of isolation, restlessness and an intense desire to be wanted and needed by someone.

The American Heritage Dictionary defines loneliness as a state of one being *"Without companions; being dejected by the awareness of being alone."* The Oxford *Advanced Learners Dictionary* defines it as a state of *"being unhappy because you have no friends or people to talk to. It is also situation or period of time that is sad and spent alone."*

Loneliness is a painful feeling of the awareness that you are not feeling connected to others and important needs are not being met. It is also the possibility of feeling excluded from a group, unloved by those around you. Lonely people feel alienated from their surroundings. There is no one to share your personal concerns and experiences with. You are finding it difficult to make friends beyond mere acquaintances.

By God's design we have an innate need to be loved and to belong. As children we learn to give and receive affection and are taught the skills that will help us find acceptance in society. Through our relationships with family, friends, co-workers and others, we form our sense of individuality and find our place in the mosaic of life. It's when that need for affection and fellowship goes unfulfilled, that we become restless, unhappy and lonely.

It is a feeling and awareness that intimacy, understanding, friendship and acceptance are missing from one's life. If unchecked on time, it may lead to depression due to the inability to cope with the fact of life. It is a feeling, a state of isolation or separation from others.

Research shows that there are basically three kinds of loneliness. These are emotional, social and existential. Emotional loneliness involves a lack of a psychologically intimate relationship with another person or persons. This kind of loneliness is what makes many singles rush into marriage in search of solution. Social loneliness is the feeling of aimlessness, anxiety and emptiness, while existential loneliness is the sense of isolation which comes to someone who is separated from God and feels that life has no meaning.

To find a permanent solution to any situation, it has to be dealt with from the roots. To overcome loneness therefore, it is crucial to understand the root causes. What causes loneliness?

Causes Of Loneliness

Poor family relationships

The psalmist David knew this and exclaimed:

When my father and my mother forsake me, then the LORD will take me up.

Psalms 27:10

Sometimes a very poor family relationship can be a major cause of loneliness among single people. The family is designed by God to be a place of fellowship and healthy relationships. When this is lacking, usually members of such families come out to the world seeking such love. But because that kind of fellowship can only be obtained in the context of a family unit, it is usually very difficult to find it with friends. That is why even when such individuals are in the midst of many people, they still feel lonely and empty.

These days, the rate of disintegration of the family unit is very alarming and of a great concern. The family institution is under serious attack by the enemy-the devil. Recently, research on the high rate of involvement of young people in higher institutions in the occult was conducted. Result shows that poor family relationships topped the list as the reason. It is time to awake and stop this ravaging plague that seeks to destroy the future generation!

I have a mandate from God to help strengthen families! I am very passionate about this. I have a vision for the family. It gives me a burden when I see any family undergoing disintegration because it was not so from the beginning! It is my assignment and I have been involved in this for over two decades now with outstanding testimonies of restorations, all to the glory of God.

However, I have come to discover among other things that a successful family relationship ought to be prepared for, from the single years because those are foundation years. The foundation of a structure determines its strength (Psalms 11:3). I have found this to be so in my own life and family, those of my associates, many successful singles as well as many that are now married.

So, my esteemed reader, this is the foundation - laying season of your life for a strong family relationship tomorrow. Parents, you cause untold damages with your poor family relationships. This is the best time to make amends. May you act on time before it is too late!

Hostility

This has been discovered to be another major cause of loneliness, especially among young people. Hostility is a feeling of anger and bitterness that alienate others and drive them away. Loneliness can also be induced by a feeling of bitterness, most especially bitterness resulting in distrust for everyone that comes around. This could be as a result of past disappointments. It could in turn lead to a transfer of aggression to other people. The hostile person becomes a difficult person to associate with. The aloneness that results could also be a cause of loneliness.

Inability or unwillingness to communicate effectively in close relationships, including even marriages, could also result in hostility. This is a very dangerous state for anyone to be in. The end result of this is loneliness.

It is not surprising therefore, that most young people who are in this state of hostility for example, become members of the occult and other dangerous groups. Most young people in higher institutions of learning have fallen victims today. A divine rescue operation is urgently required in this regard!

Changing circumstances

Changing circumstances have become the order of the day in this changing world. A change of jobs, school, break up of a long term relationship or marriage, career change and divorce are all potential causes of loneliness. Others include change in social status or difficult financial conditions. Also, circumstantial difficulties such as widowhood, childlessness, family breakdown etc are all also possible causes of loneliness.

If you look at the story of Hannah, in 1 Samuel 1: 2, 8 you will discover that because of her childlessness she was vulnerable to loneliness, in spite of her husband's demonstrated love. Widowhood also sometimes could result in desolation as the Bible recognizes in 1 Timothy 5:5

> *Now she that is a widow indeed, and desolate, trusteth in God, and continueth in supplications and prayers night and day.*

Extended absence or physical separation from loved ones – family members separated by hundreds or thousands of miles, is also a potential cause of loneliness. This explains why most young people when they leave home for a far place, especially in pursuit of their education suffer loneliness, except they are properly mentored.

All our children after high school studied far away from home. Adequate measures had to be put in place to ensure proper, close and effective monitoring. Each of them was then able to handle, deal with and overcome loneliness each time it occurred. This helped a great deal in guiding them on the path of destiny, which is yielding great rewards today.

Spiritual causes

Estrangement from God is alienation from your maker. This is very deadly! Only the redeemed that are born again, can be free from spiritual loneliness. Sin and iniquity separates from God, hence the need to be born again and be reconciled unto God.

Salvation is the only remedy to estrangement from God. Therefore, you must be born again! Please be aware that church attendance, bearing a Christian name or having Christian parents are not the same as being born again. Salvation is accepting Jesus Christ as your personal saviour. It has to be done consciously and deliberately. If you have never done that, this is your best opportunity to do so! Please pray the salvation prayer at the back of this book right now before you continue reading.

Also, un-confessed sins can be a cause of loneliness. You should never take un-confessed sins lightly because they could have serious effect. You don't have to hide iniquity in your heart or live with un-confessed sins. Remember that God is faithful and just to forgive when we confess.

If we confess our sins, he is faithful and just to forgive us our sins, and to cleanse us from all unrighteousness.
I John. 1: 9

Other causes of spiritual loneliness are rejection by friends, colleagues, relations and loved ones, misunderstandings, even in ministry, abuse and misuse by others.

Some people in the Bible had this experience of loneliness. These include: Moses (Numbers 11:14-15; Deuteronomy 1; 9, 12), Elijah (I Kings. 19: 3-5, 10; Romans 11:3), Jeremiah (Jeremiah 15:17), David (Psalms 25:16, Psalms 102; 142:4), Paul (2 Timothy 4:9-12, 16; 1:15; Acts 15:38). There are many others. Read these scriptures carefully, don't skip them and you will be amazed. But the good news is that all these men overcame loneliness. So you also can!

Societal factors

The fast, mobile and changing society we live in does not give enough time and room for healthy relationships. Excessive television viewings, living in heavily populated cities, among other things have resulted in much less time for personal communication.

Developmental transitions, such as the translation from adolescence to early adulthood, mid life, aging etc could also cause loneliness. It may also occur after the birth of a child, after marriage or after any minor or major life events. Desiring a relationship that is not happening; living in a single person's household; low self esteem; feeling unneeded; shyness and being extremely busy are all possible causes of loneliness.

Unfulfilled Expectations

This is another major cause of loneliness for many people. These include unaccomplished goals, dreams and expectations. Disappointments and setbacks in different areas of life such as academic pusuits, business, finance, career health and so on, if not properly handled can cause loneliness.

Being in a relationship that is not working,

spinsterhood and bachelorhood are all included here. Physical illness, diseases, disabilities are all possible causes of loneliness. This also explains why some physically disabled people, experience loneliness.

Many people think that disappointments and failures mean the end of the road. They fail to remember that failure is not final. There was a young man who was not measuring up academically and was asked to repeat a particular class. Because of this setback and disappointment, he ran away from home and refused to continue his education.

Chances are, many years to come, he will forever regret the step he took. I heard of a man who had every opportunity to drop out of school but refused to do so. Rather he persisted despite all negative circumstances. He ended up as a renowned statesman.

The Truth is, until you know how to successfully handle failure and disappointments, you never know the joy of success. To be distinguished as a single, you must be able to handle failure successfully. Are you battered with unfulfilled expectations? I have got good news for you. It is usually darkness before dawn, God is about to give you a positive surprise!

The Bible says:

Rejoice not against me, O mine enemy: when I fall,

I shall arise; when I sit in darkness, the LORD shall be a light unto me.

Micah 7:8

For a just man falleth seven times, and riseth up again: but the wicked shall fall into mischief.

Proverbs 24:16

Loneliness is much more than an inconvenience. If left unchecked, there is the danger of loneliness developing into anxiety and depression. It is possible to become completely immobilized by feelings of self-pity and helplessness. Some try to mask pain by oversleeping or putting in long hours at the office.

Finally, the stress imposed by loneliness leads to a weakened immune system, heart disease and other physical ailments. The moral is clear. It's time to decide to do something about it.

There are some danger spots that singleness can breed. As singles, watch out for and be careful with these danger spots. Some of them will be enumerated briefly here before we proceed to discuss how to overcome loneliness.

Loneliness: Singleness can easily breed loneliness. Singleness can be accompanied by a feeling of non-acceptance and alienation. This is why many singles suffer from loneliness. It is crucial that you know how to overcome loneliness and we shall be dealing with that shortly.

Sexual Frustration and Pressure: Singleness can create sexual frustration and pressure. The sexual drive of singles is quite high. Sexual immorality is spreading like wild fire among young adults, but this ought not to be so! God warns against this in His word (1 Corinthians 6:18). Care must therefore be taken not to be overtaken by it.

Self-centeredness: This is a tendency towards or pre-occupation with self; developing a pattern of going it all alone. Your attention is drawn only to yourself and none other. This again is unscriptural and God frowns at it (Luke 12:19-20). If you want to make a difference as a single, you must watch against this deadly danger spot.

A Search For Identity: Everyone desires an identity, singles inclusive. This search is usually very strong during the single years. It covers all areas of life, including identity in the context of a married society. Some older singles have to deal with pressure or criticism and even misunderstanding from family and friends over the issue of marriage. This is what makes some rush into marriages, which usually hit the rocks. You must avoid these so you don't end your life in regret. If you are an older single, remember, God cannot and won't miss-manage your life! So, relax – you shall surely make it.

Having dealt with some of the danger spots of singleness, let us examine how to overcome loneliness, which is the major danger spot. What are the remedies? Remember, everyone has to deal with loneliness at one point in time or another in life. The important thing is as it comes, learn to deal with it and never allow it stay! Others who have gone ahead of you have overcome it, you also will! So, what must I do to overcome loneliness?

Remedies

Rest in God's love

Be reassured that God cares and understands you and your circumstances. God makes no assumptions concerning the well being of man. Even after creating man in His own image and likeness, God still cared enough to come into the garden to check out the welfare of the man He had created and put therein. It was in the course of doing that, that He saw the lonely, deplorable state that man was. That is why the word records in Genesis 2:18:

> *And the LORD God said, It is not good that the man should be alone; I will make him an help meet for him.*

In Hebrew 2:17, the Bible describes Jesus as a faithful and merciful High Priest:

Wherefore in all things it behooved him to be made like unto his brethren, that he might be a merciful and faithful high priest in things pertaining to God, to make reconciliation for the sins of the people.

In His large heartedness Jesus declares

Come unto me, all ye that labour and are heavy laden, and I will give you rest.

Matthew 11:28

No matter your situation or what you might be going through, remember that God created you in the first instance; you did not send yourself to this world. He, who created and sent you to this earth, cares enough to ensure your well-being. So, rest in God's love!

Cultivate an intimate relationship with God

If you are born again, you have been redeemed and have become a child of God and a member of the household of God.

For ye have not received the spirit of bondage again to fear; but ye have received the Spirit of adoption, whereby we cry, Abba, Father.

The Spirit itself beareth witness with our spirit, that we are the children of God:

And if children, then heirs; heirs of God, and joint-heirs with Christ; if so be that we suffer with him, that we may be also glorified together.

Romans 8:15-17

Again the Bible says

Casting all your care upon him; for he careth for you.

1 Peter 5:7

Just like the biological family to which you belong, where you have a unique father-mother and son relationship, it should be the same spiritually. Walk and develop a strong relationship with God, so that when loneliness knocks at the door, you already have what it takes to overcome and triumph over it. Those who have developed a strong relationship with God, never have to be downcast with loneliness of any kind.

Personally, this is my greatest secret to dealing with loneliness and I can tell you, it works! To make the most of any relationship, you must work it out, so it is with your relationship with God also.

Invest quality time in God's presence through word study, prayer, fellowship, service and witnessing to others about the love of God. This should be done continuously. Replace depressing feelings with God's everlasting truth such as 2 Timothy 4:16-17

At my first answer no man stood with me, but all men forsook me: I pray God that it may not be laid to their charge.

Notwithstanding the Lord stood with me, and strengthened me; that by me the preaching might be fully known, and that all the Gentiles might hear: and I was delivered out of the mouth of the lion.

Invest time and resources to draw closer and enrich your intimacy with God. It will sure become a productive experience with positive results (1 Kings 19:9, Daniel 10:8). You can also pray for God to provide the right person, who will encourage you and whom you can also help (Psalms 32:8, Proverbs 27:17, Ecclesiastes 4:10, 11 Corinthians 7:6).

Develop an action plan

Don't just sit down there, wishing to overcome loneliness! Wishes never produce triumph. Develop an action plan. Arise and take positive steps. Think, plan, meditate on your plans, pray about them and act based on God's leading.

For example, you can go for professional Christian counseling. The Bible says:

Where no counsel is, the people fall: but in the multitude of counselors there is safety.

Proverbs 11:14

However, ensure that you seek counsel from the right source: from godly people who have proofs and will not cancel your destiny.

Reach out to others, do some volunteer work. Do those good works that involve helping others e.g. join activity group in the church. Be aggressive, renew goals and take new risks in specific areas. Keep in mind, until you take risks, you can never reach your goals!

You could also prayerfully consider a change of job. You could travel, move and experience the wonders of God's creation. Listen to Christian music and watch inspiring movies. Read good books and engage yourself in writing. Take up hobbies. Do something. Expand your horizons.

Self inventory

One of the secrets to overcoming loneliness is to learn to take an inventory of your behavior. Are you a show-off? Domineering? Moody? A complainer? A gossip? Unreliable? Nosy? Short-tempered? A taker that doesn't know how to give? Do you build walls instead of bridges? Would you want to be a friend to someone like you?

Be sincere in your examination of yourself. The truth is, no one else can examine you like you. In the natural, if you are sick, you need a medical personnel to examine you, but spiritually it is not so.

Questions provoke thoughts and point to solutions. How can you take corrective actions, unless you ask yourself what you are doing wrong? The Bible says:

Examine yourselves, whether ye be in the faith; prove your own selves. Know ye not your own selves, how that Jesus Christ is in you, except ye be reprobates?
2 Corinthians 13: 5

If you are still mired in loneliness, that is because you are waiting to be rescued. Don't hold your breath because help isn't on the way. If you need a hand, you will only find it at the end of your own arm.

Focus on Giving, not Receiving

If you treasure people as God treasures them, you will lift them and this lifting it will rebound to you; adding fulfillment to your own life. We reap what we sow (Galatians 6:7). So, seek to give to others what you would like someone special to give to you. It is in giving that you receive. Always remember: giving precedes receiving. Only givers are permitted to be receivers.

Think of all the lonely people in hospitals, for instance, visit hospital patients and relieve their loneliness. If you wish to have a friend, you must be a friend. You have to give away what you wish to receive. Our actions are balls that bounce back to us. A corollary of that law is: Don't give others what you don't want to receive.

Therefore all things whatsoever ye would that men should do to you, do ye even so to them: for this is the law and the prophets.

Matthew 7:12

Your focus is the issue here. Those who focus on giving, triumph over loneliness, while those who focus on receiving, suffer loneliness. The choice is yours! Remember: giving is living! I practise this as a lifestyle and I can tell you it brings great refreshing.

Accept responsibility

Stop blaming your loneliness on others, because as long as you do, you remain on the same spot. Rather, start taking responsibility for the choices you make. It is time to make the right choices. You deserve to be happy. So, take the steps that will pull you out of the gutter of loneliness.

Blame is self-defeating. Responsibility is self-actualizing. You cannot overcome loneliness, until you are ready to accept responsibility. Live by the precept: If it is to be, it is up to me.

Focus on the positive

If you don't have any friends, look in the mirror and what do you see? A smile or a frown? If you walk around with a chip on your shoulder, you drive people away. Conversely, if you are polite and friendly, you attract others to yourself.

People instinctively sidestep a person whose unsmiling face suggests he or she might be grumpy or angry or preoccupied. It makes them wary, heightening their own fear of rejection. Alternatively, when someone with a smile catches their eye, their defenses drop and they feel drawn to the person. They find themselves thinking: 'Here is someone who will accept me; someone I can feel comfortable with.'

If you wish to attract birds, scatter bread crumbs, if you wish to attract friends, scatter seeds of love.

Exercise

Loneliness is a state of passivity. To erase it, you need to be active. Get involved in an exercise programme. Exercise will make you feel better by improving your health, lifting your spirits and boosting your confidence. And while doing so, you may make new friends.

As you put these to work, I welcome you to your season of triumph over the deadly thing called loneliness.

13
Chapter 13

SPINSTERHOOD, BACHELORHOOD AND FAMILY PRESSURE

Seek ye out of the book of the Lord, and read: no one of these shall fail, none shall want her mate:
Isaiah 34:16

It is often common to find in our society today, a situation where spinsters and bachelors are virtually castigated and ostracized by reason of their status. Their situation is being considered as abnormal. These bachelors and spinsters are made to feel the pulse and the vibe of this society, everywhere they seem to turn.

Research shows that over the past thirty (30) years, single adults are a rapidly growing into a segment of our society and of the Christian community. This explains why this chapter is crucial in this material.

The *American Heritage Dictionary* defines a spinster as *"A woman who has remained single beyond the conventional age for marrying."* While a bachelor is simply defined as: *"An unmarried man."* Spinsterhood or Bachelorhood is therefore, a state or a phase of life, for males and females, who conventionally have grown beyond the age of marriage. This means they are older than the average young single person.

It is usually a challenging period for such singles. They are faced with a unique set of pressures, characterized by mixed and troubling emotions. They are often faced with, not only questions such as: 'Will I ever get married? What if…? And what if…? These are questions that seem to have no end. Most people in this category face a lot of family and societal pressures.

I want to begin this chapter by saying to such people, please be aware that delay is not equal to denial! God is about to give you the greatest positive surprise of your life, as long as you hold on to His word!

If you are single now and people think you have passed the conventional age of marriage, it could be so in the eyes of the people of the world, but there is good news for you. If you desire to be married, the only wise God says: *"none shall want her mate"* (Isaiah 34:16). Therefore, rejoice and ask yourself what step you need to take, for your spouse to locate you.

Spinsterhood and bachelorhood could be caused by the lack of a suitor, indecision, fear and a host of other issues. It could even be by choice: some choose to be single all their lifetime due to personal reasons! Whatever the reason, this category of people, usually face a lot of pressure especially from the family.

Why is there family pressure during spinsterhood and bachelorhood?

Many families and most people in the society see spinsterhood or bachelorhood as a shame. They see it as a shame for a marriageable single that is advanced in age, to remain unmarried. Some parents at this time, start comparing themselves with their mates, who are already grandparents. Some become apprehensive, wanting to see their grand children and have in-laws. So, they start laying pressure on their unmarried adult children. I come in contact with such parents often and you could see the anxiety in them.

Pressure also comes from the family on spinsters and bachelors when their colleagues, childhood friends and sometimes even younger ones get married and or start having children. At this point, some family members start asking all kinds of questions. This situation can create a lot of discomfort for these singles.

Some parents see their children who are spinsters and bachelors as burdens; therefore, they put pressure on them to get married. Because of such pressure, some older singles especially the ladies weep all night and live a life of discomfort. Some see themselves as failures and find it difficult to believe they could ever make it in life. Such singles only help the family confirm their fear of their daughter or son would never getting married.

Shame, generally is a universal citizen. It resides in every country of the world. It knows neither race nor colour. It must be dealt with if you are to enjoy the blessedness of your relationship with God. You can be free from shame. As a spinster or bachelor, you may have experienced some difficulty in settling down. Everything may have seem to have been turned upside down. Remember the word of the Lord to you:

> *For your shame ye shall have double; and for confusion they shall rejoice in their portion: therefore in their land they shall possess the double: everlasting joy shall be unto them.*
>
> Isaiah 61: 7

How do I handle family pressure as a spinster or bachelor? You may ask. This will be examined shortly, but before that, there are certain danger spots that must be guided against at this stage of life.

Beware Of These Danger Sports!

Eagerness

This is very common among older singles. It is a

danger spot that you need to beware of. This fear, real or imagined, moves them to make hasty choices, without considering the long term effect. How do you know if you are eager to get married? Consider these useful hints:

- Intense pre-occupation with wanting to get married.

- Emotional inconsistency depending on the existence or absence of a relationship.

- Declining of interest in spiritual matters.

- Withdrawal from others – friends, family, colleagues, etc.

Excessive mindfulness of looks and appearance.

The bible says:

> *...he that believeth shall not make haste.*
>
> Isaiah 28:16

In other words, haste is associated with unbelief. Beware! Don't because of eagerness lose your colourful destiny. Trust God to bring to pass his will concerning you, at His own time and concentrate on the positive things of life.

Assumption And Misinterpreting Closeness or Friendliness.

Due to pressure at this particular time, it is very easy to assume and misinterpret closeness or friendliness.

Never assume a relationship! That someone is being polite and friendly towards you, does not necessarily mean that such a one has a marriage intention.

A relationship that will lead to marriage has to be consciously entered into by both parties. Never assume a relationship simply on the basis of proximity! That is why I want to plead with men not to keep giving particular ladies special attention to the exclusion of others, when there is nothing going on between you. Usually, I advise ladies, to politely ask for clarification in such cases, so as to avoid assumptions, which may lead to regrets in future. Don't ever misinterpret closeness or friendliness for marriage intentions.

Rushing Into Marriage

A wise man once said: 'The best of God cannot be rushed!' This is very true. Spinsters and bachelors are usually faced with the danger of wanting to rush to marry anyone that comes along, having waited for a long period of time. It is not wisdom rushing into marriage simply because you have found a Christian man and woman; it may lead to an error that you will live to regret. The reason is what makes marriage last, among other things, is character and it cannot be discerned in a hurry!

You need to give your relationship some time in order

to prove the sincerity of the other person. Having waited for a long time, does not make 'just anyone that comes along' good enough for you. So, be patient! Remember that the bible says:

For the inward thought and the heart of a man are deep.
Psalms 64:6 (NIS)

Some of the other reasons spinsters and bachelors rush into marriage include: Problems with parents or guardians, comparing oneself with colleagues and friends, challenges from friends and family, the desire to spite a former partner, accommodation problems and so on. You need to beware so as not to fall into any of those.

Pre-Marital Sex

Some older singles involve themselves in pre-marital sex, thinking that it is way to compel their partners to marry them. Nothing could be farther from the truth and more disastrous than that! Don't buy into that lie of the devil, perpetrated by satanic beliefs today. In most cases, lifetime regret is usually the end result. Some even end up having pre-marital sex with several people.

To avoid this pitfall, discipline your mind and body. Don't feed on sexually arousing materials, so you don't stir up sexual fires. You must understand that sex alone will never make a man or woman stay committed to you; in fact, it destroys commitment. The bible says:

Flee fornication. Every sin that a man doeth is without the body; but he that committeth fornication sinneth against his own body.

I Corinthians 6:18

Sex is not just a physical thing; it involves the whole of you. Sleeping with someone involves giving a part of you each time and cutting covenants with them. No wonder, many people find it difficult to connect and be truly intimate with their spouses after marriage because of pre-marital sex.

It is not only that. Trust, which is a most vital aspect of marriage, is destroyed. So also is respect. What a price to pay for just a few moments of hurried "enjoyment"!

Worry

One major pitfall that you must beware of as an older single is worry. Worry always makes you sorry. When you feel sorry for yourself, you end up with sorrow and sorrow of course leads to a broken heart. You have only one heart, why must you allow sorrow to break it for you? Or do you have a spare one?

You hear some people say things such as: "I have been born again; doing everything my Pastor says I should do, how long will I wait? Everybody else in my family of my age is married except me." Before long, he/she begins to feel sorry for himself or herself and the head is cast down. Such people begin to look older than their age. At the age of thirty-five, they look like fifty-five. Why? Worry! Please stop worrying!

One other thing that worry does is to tie you to your past. May be as unbelievers you have been in a relationship, but now you begin to regret and say, "I wish I did not break that relationship." You are tied to your past, and if you are not careful, you will pass with the past! Rather than tying your present to the past, let go of the past, so you can take hold of the key of today and unlock the great tomorrow that God has in store for you.

Worry ties you to your past and as long as you are tied to your past, you remain stagnated, you are not moving forward: and as long as you are not moving forward, you never reach unto your great tomorrow!

Jesus said,

> *Which of you by taking thought can add one cubit unto his stature?*
>
> Matthew 6:27

If you cannot, then it is not wise to get worried. From today, I see every worry in your life come to an end!

Do you know that for worrying, a lot of people lie down in bed at night but, sleep is far from their eyes?

They go to church, sing and dance; but when they get back home; it is back to square one for them. Before you know it, a robust man begins to lose weight fast. You think he is on a diet, but it is a worry diet for him!

Worry can lead to weight loss. When you start thinking and thinking, you are tied to your past and before you know what is happening, you lose appetite! Please watch it! Worrying has adverse effects! If you don't control it, it tends to get out of control!

A single lady is over concerned about her future until every good man passes her by. She is so worried that she is never happy; she is always morose. Even when God tells a man to go near her and the man comes, he says, "This one that never smiles, can I be a husband to her? God please oh! I don't think I can handle her! Show me another one." As you begin to brighten up, I see God bring you a man/woman after His own heart, in Jesus' name!

Jealousy

Jealousy is a dangerous pitfall and many spinsters and bachelors have been victims of it. How does jealousy come? It comes when you feel others are getting ahead of you. You see your colleagues moving ahead of you and you feel bad. You are filled with thoughts such as: "We finished school together, now look at him/her married with children and I am still single!"

Irritability is one of the signs of jealousy. Some older singles become easily irritable, especially when they see their colleagues married. Rather than rejoice with them, so that their miracle can become real on time, they get irritable and become unfriendly to such people. Instead of feeling jealous, find out what others are doing that you are not doing right and change your attitude and things will change for the better for you as well!

Jealousy can come from a feeling of insecurity. Whenever others outshine you, you feel threatened. You get afraid that such persons will soon be more popular and better placed in life than you. Such a person could be in your service group in the church, at your place of work, etc.

Jealousy can also come out of comparison. Who are you comparing yourself with?

> *For we dare not make ourselves of the number, or compare ourselves with some that commend themselves: but they measuring themselves by themselves, and comparing themselves among themselves, are not wise.*
>
> 2 Corinthians 10:12

Don't you know that you are uniquely made by God? There is a part of God that only you can fulfill. That is why God said in 1 Peter 2:9, *"But ye are a chosen generation, a royal priesthood, an holy nation, a peculiar people; that ye should show forth the praises of him who hath called you out of darkness into his marvellous light."*

You are chosen; you are peculiar and the word peculiar means that you are in a class of your own; you just stand out! So, don't keep comparing yourself with others, so you don't miss your unique identity. Otherwise, you will live all your life as a copy, when God made you an original!

Stop comparing yourself with others, ask God to reveal you to you and then live as you, set to fulfill destiny standing out and shining where God has placed you. Convince yourself: "I may not be married yet, but I will get there!"

Finally, jealousy comes out of envy. Remember Cain and Abel: Because of envy, God accepted the offering of Abel and rejected that of Cain. You will not lose out! Give no room to envy or else you will end up in the pit.

Anger

This is another danger spot that older singles must beware of. Anger comes out of a feeling of displeasure. When you are displeased about something, you get angry. It also comes out of indignation, hostility and ultimately degenerates into wrath.

Some older singles get angry when their mates get married. Others even get angry at God! The truth is, if you are angry at God who then will help you? Really, anger puts you farther away from God and thereby farther from your miracle.

Having considered these danger spots to be avoided, let us now examine how to handle family pressure.

How To Handle Family Pressure

Set Your Life Priorities Right

First and foremost, you must locate what God wants for the fulfillment of your destiny. Pursue it with all vehemence, you must not allow the desire to get married rob you of your reason for existence. That will be a misplaced priority. Some people struggle, run and sweat, but in most cases, with little or no result, such people often misplace their priorities! If I may ask you, what are your priorities and what are you living for? The Bible says you should not be as the horse or as the mule, which have no understanding (Psalms 32:9).

What you treasure reveals what your real priorities are. Judah (Haggai 1 & 2), like many of us had confused priorities with those things we think or place first over God: such as career, marriage, vacation and many such activities that take us away from God. Too often the most important- God- is left at the rear. Values are misplaced!

What is your essence of living? Marriage is important,

but it is not everything. Why are you on the surface of the earth? What does God require of you in order to have a fulfilled life? Of course, you must be aware that marriage is not equal to automatic fulfillment in life. There are many who are married but are far from being fulfilled. Learn to set your priorities correctly, putting first things first if you must overcome family pressure. The word of God says:

> *But seek ye first the kingdom of God, and his righteousness; and all these things shall be added unto you.*
>
> Matthew 6:33

When your priorities are correctly placed, it becomes difficult if not impossible, for you to be distracted due to pressure. You must set your priorities right if you must live a life that is free from family pressure as an older single. You will make it!

Give God His Rightful Place in Your Life

For you to overcome family pressure and get to the place where God has destined for you in life, you must give God his rightful place in your own life first. How do I do this, you may ask?

Fear The Lord: This, the Bible says is the whole, not part; but the whole duty of man!

And now, Israel, what doth the LORD thy God

require of thee, but to fear the LORD thy God, to walk in all his ways, and to love him, and to serve the LORD thy God with all thy heart and with all thy soul,

Deuteronomy 10:12

This is what God requires of everyone. Do you have the fear of the Lord? Do you have time to seek out of the book of the law to know God's requirement for your fulfilled life?

Fear in this context connotes respect and reverence for God and His word. It is not about being afraid because you are His child. Whatever He says should be your guiding principle. Walk in the understanding that you have God as your head, who watches over you. He notices your doings and movements. So, whatever He tells you to do, you must do it without questions or grumbling.

Those who fear God don't fear men; rather, men fear them!

Walk In His Ways: Until you are determined to walk in God's ways, irrespective of your situation as an older single, you cannot be free from family pressure. The bible says:

And thine ears shall hear a word behind thee, saying, This is the way, walk ye in it, when ye turn to the right hand, and when ye turn to the left.

Isaiah 30:21

Before you can walk in God's ways, you must respect and reverence Him. Whenever He says turn to the right, you don't turn to the left. When He commands you to wait, you will not get impatient and start moving. His ways are far better than your ways. It might not look like what you feel it should be, but His ways will not lead to a dead end. The scripture puts it very clearly that:

> *There is a way which seemeth right unto a man, but the end thereof are the ways of death.*
>
> Proverbs 14:1

Love God: If you truly give God His rightful place in your life, you will love Him unreservedly.

> *And thou shalt love the Lord thy God with all thy heart, and with all thy soul, and with all thy mind, and with all thy strength: this is the first commandment.*
>
> Mark 12:30

God requires your love. Your love for Him must be sincere, not just in words but let your action show that you love Him. If you love Him deep down in your heart, He will lead you into the center of His will where you will find pleasure.

Your love for Him must be seen by all your family members. Let the world see that you are lost in His love. This will diffuse all the pressures around you.

Engage In Kingdom Service

Kingdom service is another major key here. Addiction

to kingdom service frees you from pressure and positions you for your desired miracle. The Bible says:

And ye shall serve the Lord your God, and he shall bless...

Exodus 23:25

What positions you for marital blessing is kingdom service. God does not only require you to fear, love and walk with Him, He also requires that you serve Him. Service will occupy you and you will be less worried about your situation. The story of Ruth the Moabite in the Bible is an example, of how service can distinguish you for marital blessing.

In the case of Ruth, she was a young widow; a stranger in the land (Israel) and living with an old widow who had lost her two sons. But she keyed into the instruction of her mother in-law. She got a location to glean and there she was noticed by the man who eventually became her husband.

Then said Boaz unto his servant that was set over the reapers, Whose damsel is this?

And the servant that was set over the reapers answered and said, It is the Moabitish damsel that came back with Naomi out of the country of Moab:

Ruth 2:5-6

Your place of service is a fertile ground, where your

miracle can easily reach you. My husband located me in a place of service, many years ago!

Are you involved in kingdom service? Don't just sit down and occupy a seat in church, contributing nothing! It gets people frustrated. Find a place of service. Get involved and serve God acceptably.

How do you serve God acceptably? Heartily! You can not genuinely serve somebody you do not love. When your love is in place for God, you will willingly serve Him with your being. Your miracle testimony is the next!

Refuse Anxiety

When the family begins to mount pressure on an eligible spinster or bachelor, he/she can easily fall into a state of anxiety. But the good news is that you can refuse anxiety. However, for you to be able to do so, you must have an understanding of what anxiety is and the negative effect it can have on you.

Anxiety, according to the *Cambridge Advanced Learner's Dictionary* is defined as an uncomfortable feeling of nervousness or worry about something that is happening or might happen in future; or something that causes a feeling of fear and worry.

Anxiety has its root in fear which is the opposite of faith. It is a universal killer disease, which cannot be cured by medication! John Mueller said "the beginning of anxiety is the end of faith and the end of anxiety is the beginning of faith." Without faith the writer of the book of Hebrews says, it is impossible to please God (Hebrews 11:6). That is to say, you cannot please God in this state of anxiety.

The effect of anxiety can be devastating. Spiritually, it can cut off your relationship with God and take away your joy. Without joy, you cannot worship God, neither can you serve Him acceptably, nor pray effectively. Physically, if left unchecked, it degenerates into physically dangerous diseases. With all these, the devil has a free hand to operate and anything could happen. Fight anxiety and get free from it. Give the devil no place in your life.

If anxiety is so deadly especially for older singles, is there any cure for it? How can I deal with it? How can I refuse it?

Cure For Anxiety

The only cure for anxiety is the word of God. The word is the never failing solution to every issues of life. Hebrews 1:3 says,

> **Who being the brightness of his glory, and the express image of his person, and upholding all things by the word of his power, ...**

God's commandment for the cure for anxiety is well

stated in the scriptures:

Be careful for nothing; but in every thing by prayer and supplication with thanksgiving let your requests be made known unto God.

Philippians 4:6

This scripture is a commandment from God. To obey is better than sacrifice. When you give room to anxiety, you are walking in disobedience. You may say: 'well, I know it is a commandment, but what can I do now in my present condition? My mates are already married, my little sisters and cousins are getting married and no man has asked my hand in marriage, I am gradually approaching 40years.'

God knows about all these before He said you should be anxious for nothing. The book of Proverbs 29:1 says: *He, that being often reproved hardeneth his neck, shall suddenly be destroyed, and that without remedy.*

Anyone who refuses instructions shall perish suddenly without remedy. God has given you what it takes to deal with anxiety. You have the power to refuse anxiety. When you consciously refuse to be anxious, you are obeying God and He in turn, begins to make things work out favourably for you.

When you are given to anxiety, you are judging God unfaithful and you are calling Him a liar. You are not sure of His abilities and therefore, you can no more depend on Him. This is a grievous sin. Free yourself of the entanglement of anxiety today and give God a chance in your affairs. You can refuse anxiety! But how? You may ask. Carefully consider the following:

Be Given To Prayer: The Bible says:

> *Casting all your care upon him; for he careth for you.*
>
> 1 Peter 5:7

One major way of getting God committed in your affairs is by committing your ways to Him in prayer. It is true that prayer changes things and it is the master key as we commonly declare, but do we apply this principle in our lives?

> *Commit thy way unto the Lord; trust also in him; and he shall bring it to pass.*
>
> Psalms 37:5

The family pressure can be taken to God in prayer. Pray to the Father in the name of Jesus. Nothing is too small to take to God in prayer, after all He is your heavenly Father and He can do all things. Pour out your heart to Him. The children of Israel cried out to God in the land of their bondage and He heard them.

> *And the Lord said, I have surely seen the affliction of my people which are in Egypt, and have heard their cry by reason of their taskmasters; for I know their sorrows;*

And I am come down to deliver them out of the hand of the Egyptians, and to bring them up out of that land unto a good land and a large, unto a land flowing with milk and honey; unto the place of the Canaanites, and the Hittites, and the Amorites, and the Perizzites, and the Hivites, and the Jebusites.

Now therefore, behold, the cry of the children of Israel is come unto me: and I have also seen the oppression wherewith the Egyptians oppress them.

Exodus 3:7-9

God is waiting to hear your voice in prayers, not in worrying. Concerning marital disappointment; your advancement in age without a suitor should not provoke worry, rather it should make you to take it to God in prayers. No amount of worry has ever solved any problem; rather, it compounds issues.

If you have received the baptism of the Holy Spirit, pray in the Spirit more and if you have not, seek the baptism of the Holy Spirit with the evidence of speaking in tongues. Those who are prayerful are usually anxiety free!

Supplication: This is a very important secret to overcoming anxiety. The Bible says:

And give him no rest, till he establish, and till he make Jerusalem a praise in the earth.

Isaiah 62:7

Supplication is a higher form of prayer. It passes the

level of just waiting until a matter takes its course. This is a level whereby you seek His face more earnestly. Petition the Lord by putting together relevant scriptures that apply to your situation. Reasoning with God in His word: Hannah did this and she received her heart's desire. Travail in purposeful; targeted prayer and you will be surprised how easily you can refuse anxiety and how fast your awaited spouse will show up!

Engage In Heart-Felt Thanksgiving: This is very crucial!

> *Let the people praise thee, O God; let all the people praise thee. Then shall the earth yield her increase; and God, even our own God, shall bless us. God shall bless us; and all the ends of the earth shall fear him.*
>
> Psalms 67:5-7

If you want to come out of this prolonged pressure and a state of being single: begin to give quality thanks to God. Give no room to murmuring or complaining (1 Corinthians 10:10, Numbers 11:1). Look away from the mockery of men! Remember, it was thanksgiving that brought Lazarus out of the grave.

Fill your heart and mouth with His praises. Dance, sing, rejoice and make the devil mad! This should not be only when you are in church or people are around, but much more when you are alone. Sing in your understanding and in the spirit! Never point an accusing finger at God concerning your situation. The bible says:

> *Although the fig tree shall not blossom, neither shall fruit be in the vines; the labour of the olive shall fail, and the fields shall yield no meat; the flock shall be cut off from the fold, and there shall be no herd in the stalls: Yet I will rejoice in the Lord, I will joy in the God of my salvation.*
>
> Habakkuk 3:17-18

Be full of joy and praise and you will see Him in action. You easily overcome family pressure by dealing a deadly blow on anxiety, that way attract your miracle quickly.

One man from our church gave this testimony. "I had believed God for a wife because I was tired of loneliness. I was present at one of the Hosanna Nights, where the Bishop said we should write whatever represented a problem in our lives on a piece of paper and dance over it. I wrote that God should make me a husband before the end of that year. That night, I danced my way out of loneliness, and now I am married!" Isn't God wonderful?

A lady also gave this testimony in church sometime ago. She was 45(forty-five) years old and was single. When she understood the miracle power in praise, she began to give God thanks even in her situation.

According to her, on a particular day, she gave God thanks seven thousand (7,000) times. Miraculously, her husband showed up! When she came up to give her testimony, she was already covenantly and gloriously married.

By the special grace of God, as you take the three steps above, your own testimony shall be the next!

Keep Your Hopes Up!

To handle pressures from various quarters as an older single, you must learn to keep your hopes up. When you become hopeless on any issue, you become helpless. To enjoy the help of God therefore, you must be full of hope.

The Bible says:

> *For to him that is joined to all the living there is hope: for a living dog is better than a dead lion.*
>
> Ecclesiastes 9: 4

When you are in Christ, you are joined to the living and therefore have hope. What if I keep my hope up and it does not produce result as expected? You may ask. But, what if it does? And really, it usually does! I can assure you. Your case is not hopeless! Your case is not closed because there is no closed case with God.

> *I am the vine, ye are the branches: He that abideth in me, and I in him, the same bringeth forth much*

fruit: for without me ye can do nothing.

John 15:5

As long as you are connected to the Vine in the person of Jesus Christ, the devil cannot close your case. God's plan for you is to give you a future and a hope (Jeremiah 29:11).

Stop asking God questions such as: Why me? Where are you Lord? Can I still depend on you and your word? Are you still there? Am I not getting too old for marriage? But when will you answer me, Lord? These are questions of hopelessness.

When you give room to hopelessness in any situation, worry and sorrow set in and before you know it your head is cast down. When you are worried, the devil wearies you. Sorrow makes you feel sorry. This in turn lead to depression. You cannot be oppressed, until you are depressed. Jesus came to free you from all oppressions of the devil (Acts 10:38). You must come out of your shell of depression and everything that seeks to cast you down, by celebrating the redemptive benefits in your life!

Refuse to be offended at God, no matter the pressure (Luke 7:23). Never react negatively to God because of your condition so you don't become helpless. Never justify yourself against God. Don't be angry at God else, you may get stranded in life. Many old singles are stranded just because of this. He is your only helper who can dignify your life.

Also, you must ensure that you do not follow any other god in search of a marriage partner. Any alternative god you follow in search of a spouse, will definitely expose your nakedness in life. Don't try it! God is more than enough. He is too faithful to fail, He is dependable and He is more than enough!

Recognize That God Is Not Slow!

Let this become your watchword. Remember the word of God says:

> *God is not a man, that he should lie; neither the son of man, that he should repent: hath he said, and shall he not do it? or hath he spoken, and shall he not make it good?*

Numbers 23:19

As you are expecting your life partner, look unto God. Never be too fast for Him, His own time is the right time. Those who choose to look unto God never see shame (Psalms 34:5). Looking unto God means finding out what His word says about your situation and applying yourself to it. As you do this without wavering, every shame shall be rolled away, giving room to honour for you.

The Psalmist cried:

Let my heart be sound in thy statutes; that I be not ashamed.

Psalms 119:80

The statutes of God are His commandment. In order to be free from shame and reproach, the Psalmist says your heart must be sound in God's word. When you lay up His word in your heart, you shall be built up.

When the Word is laid up in your heart, it shall find expression in your mouth and you receive whatever you say. When you talk negative, you see negative. When you talk positive you see positive.

Refuse every other alternative; make Him the source of your help in all your endeavours. The Bible says anyone that makes man the source of his help, shall end up in misery (Jeremiah 17: 5-6). That shall be minus you in Jesus' name.

Put Your Emotions Under Control

To effectively handle pressure as an older single, you must put your emotions under control. Every human being whether male or female has emotions, but these emotions are not meant to control us but to complement our lives. For uncontrolled emotions, many singles have missed their 'would- be' spouses.

What are emotions? You may ask. Emotions can be described as strong instinctive feelings and they include feeling such as love, hate, fear, anxiety, worries, pride, comparison etc. Many relationships have been ruined for lack of controlled emotions. Do you know that many singles have missed their 'would- be spouses for lack of emotional control?

The Bible says:

> To every thing there is a season, and a time to every purpose under the heaven:
>
> A time to weep, and a time to laugh; a time to mourn, and a time to dance;
>
> Ecclesiastes 3:1 & 4

That talks about emotions. Emotions are a part and parcel of you, God created you with emotions, so in themselves, emotions are not evil. It is the handling of them that determines what they produces in you.

Your emotions determine your attitude and your attitude determines your altitude or how far you go in life. Many people with negative attitudes are victims of uncontrolled emotions.

For example, a man who allows his single status take a hold on him and affect his attitude in his place of work, if he may soon lose his job, not because of the devil, mind you, but because he left his emotions unchecked.

What about the one who carries a long face because all her mates are married and she is not. She may even be thinking, 'what is God still doing?' I don't miss church, I serve him faithfully; what else am I supposed to do?' She may not tell anyone, but her emotions are moving her towards a dead end.

Before you know it, rather than dancing and rejoicing, she begins to shed tears. Someone asks 'why?' The answer is uncontrolled emotions! So instead of bringing God's blessing closer, she succeeds in pushing them farther. The devil would say, 'You have done everything better than those who are standing there with their husbands.'

Yes, that is the truth! But better take it easy! If you are offended in God, who will help you? However, like I often say humorously, in case you really think that God has hurt you, please forgive Him!

If my emotions are this important, how do I put them under control? You may ask. Let us briefly examine this here.

How to put your emotions under control

Renew Your Mind by the Word of God

The Word of God is the principal raw material for the renewal of the mind (Colossians 3:10). You need to read the Word by yourself every day until your mind is saturated with the Word. Listen to and watch Bible-based Christian messages. Read Bible-based books that can help purify your mind.

Beware of Junk

Beware of those books, magazines, and musical tapes, audio and video CD's that you bought before you got born again. Be careful with those movies that you watch secretly! The earlier you stop watching them the better for you.

Who do you think you are deceiving? As it is said in the computer world: garbage in, garbage out! What you feed your mind on will reflect in your emotions. In other words, if you feed your mind with junk, you will live a junk life. You need to be careful what you load your mind with. Those things need to become part of the old things that must pass in your life so you don't pass with them. You need to destroy them!

Learn Instant Forgiveness

Maybe somebody did you wrong: you can't undo that wrong, so the wisest thing is to forgive instantly and move on. Don't wait until the person comes to apologize. If he or she doesn't come to ask for forgiveness until Jesus comes, will you want to go to hell because of someone? Don't let your destination be terminated by anybody! Before anybody wrongs you, forgive the person. That is what my husband calls it 'advance forgiveness'. Those who practise instant forgiveness are able to easily control their emotions.

However, if someone offends you, it is important for you to call the person and let him know that what he did offended you, so that he won't repeat it. Whether such a person agrees and apologizes or not should not affect you negatively. But, don't hold any grudge against anyone. If you do, it could break your heart, and you don't have a spare! You will not have a broken heart, in Jesus' name.

Learn Contentment

To be able to control your emotions, you must learn contentment. You don't have any reason to compare yourself with any other person. Remember, godliness with contentment is great gain (1 Timothy 6:6) and that life is in phases and men are in sizes. The phase you are right now is for your good. Handle it well and you will progress to a better phase tomorrow. You are single today, but the 'single days' are a phase in your life; it will soon become history and a testimony!

Use the Weapon of Prayer

You can control your emotions easily by putting the weapon of prayer to work.

Philippians 4:6 says:

Be careful for nothing; but in every thing by prayer

and supplication with thanksgiving let your requests
be made known unto God.

When you have greater things than you can handle, remember that you have a great God with whom all things are possible and you have a great High Priest, in the person of Jesus.

So, learn to put your emotions under control by renewing your mind by the word of God, avoiding feeding your soul with junk and unedifying information also refuse to sit in the midst of the scornful and all those who constantly put you under pressure and constant reminder of your position. If you can put your emotions in check, you will also be able to wade off the pressure on you.

Whatever you have lost in the past for uncontrolled emotions, God will not only restore back, but according to Isaiah 60:7, He will give you double. So, welcome to your season of double restoration!

Single For Life?

There are examples, both in the Bible and in our contemporary world of people who were never married, were widowed and yet made full proof of their purpose and calling in life. There are also great people who live as celibates. That a person is single does not necessarily mean he or she cannot fulfill the ultimate of his or her life here on earth.

It is not impossible to have some people who have chosen to be single all their life time. This chapter will not be complete without a word concerning such people. Let me quickly mention here that it is not unscriptural to remain single for life. However, if you are making this choice, you must ensure that you can faithfully abide by it. Your singleness must be for God's glory. Also, it is important to ensure that purity is maintained so you can make heaven at the end of your journey on earth.

Some Biblical examples of successful singles include Elijah, Elisha, Daniel, Anna (Luke 2:27-37), Paul, Jeremiah (Jeremiah 16:2), Philips' four daughters (Acts 21:9), Shadrach, Meshach, Abednego, Mary, Martha and Lazarus. Also, Paul's missionary co-workers such as Silas, Luke, Apollos, Lydia and Phoebe were all singles.

In our contemporary world, examples of successful singles include Thomas Aquinas, Saint Francis of Assisi, the British Theologian John Stott. C.S. Lewis, one of the greatest leaders of church history was a bachelor most of his life. He married at age 57 for four years only and remained celibate after his wife's death. Others include Teresa of Avla, Joan of Arc and Thomas A. Kempis.

To such people God has promised everlasting name if they serve Him (Isaiah 56: 3-5). Ensure that you make productive use of your single years by investing into destinies and God will make you a name and praise upon the earth!

However, if your being single is not your choice and you desire to be married but it seems things are not working out the way you expected, don't lose hope because this is your season of remembrance and God will remember you for good! Your case is not impossible for God to handle. Expect a miracle from God!

"23 years marital stagnation destroyed"! This was the title of a sister's testimony in our church. According to her, God supernaturally stepped into her case. Despite all the challenges that came up, God fulfilled His word and she got married in December 2004.

A brother titled his testimony "God dazed me". He had an embarrassing marital problem. According to him, he experienced six broken engagements that could not be explained. The last one took place after the wedding date had been fixed and invitation cards distributed. But by divine intervention, he was transferred in his work place to another city where he met his covenant wife. Now he is gloriously married.

Your story will change for the better! Right now, I

decree your release from every marital entanglement, in Jesus name! Experience a divine positive turnaround of your situation culminating in the fulfillment of your marital desires. It is done in Jesus' name. So, begin to give God thanks. You shall make it!

14

Chapter 14

Preparing For Marriage

It has been a most exciting adventure travelling through this material. The work in this book however, cannot be concluded, without considering the all important subject, of how a single that has made a difference should prepare for marriage. Without any doubt, a distinguished single life is a sure foundation for a glorious marriage. If you commit yourself to the practice of the fundamental issues discussed in the preceding chapters, you will have without any doubt laid a strong foundation for a great marriage.

However, you cannot live in a foundation; so these fundamentals alone are not enough. Other indispensable issues are required to be put in place before you can enjoy a glorious marriage.

Marital bliss is the desire of every distinguished single who intends to marry. But, every great event is a product of a great preparation. Marriage, you must understand, is a life-time journey! So, a great preparation is required so as to enjoy a great marriage.

The Bible records:

So Jotham became mighty, because he prepared his ways before the LORD his God.

2 Chronicles 27:6

The secret of Jotham's might is traceable to his level of preparation. A wise man once said, *"Proper preparation prevents poor performance."* In other words, the quality of your performance is determined by your preparation. To have an outstanding performance, you must of necessity prepare properly!

The *American Heritage Dictionary* defines 'prepare' as, *"to make ready beforehand for a specific purpose, as for an event or occasion."* To have an eventful marriage therefore, certain things must be made ready before hand. Don't just get married as a green horn – without adequate preparation for the life ahead.

Many singles prepare for wedding without preparing for marriage. This is dangerous! Understand that wedding is different from marriage: one precedes the other but both require adequate preparation to avoid disappointment, shame and disgrace in future.

Worthy of note also is the fact that it is possible to have a great wedding ceremony without a great marriage! There are people who had societal weddings, I am aware, but never experienced marital success. Some of such marriages have ended in regret, separation, divorce and unhappiness. But how? You may ask. Follow this carefully.

A wedding is a ceremony, an event. An event, as you know comes and goes. This explains why the popular phrase: 'wedding ceremony.' Marriage, on the other hand is a union; it is the coming together of two people of opposite sex, with a view to building a God-centred home. One man, one woman; it is the union of spirit, soul and body (Genesis 2:24). It actually involves a higher level of relationship with each other, than with any other person on earth.

Preparation for marriage begins before preparation for a wedding ceremony. Wedding preparation is just a part of preparation for marriage. A wedding ceremony usually precedes the consummation of a marriage. So, preparation for marriage leads to preparation for wedding, which eventually culminates in the consummation of a union between a husband and wife.

Both wedding and marriage require adequate preparation. It is amazing, how much time people spend preparing for a ceremony that will last for just a couple of hours, without paying adequate attention to the lifetime that lies ahead after the ceremony. In everyday life, people invest a lot of time and money preparing and learning how to be successful in business, career, vocations, etc; yet little or nothing is invested into preparing for a great marriage which is a life time journey. This explains why more marriages are breaking down today than ever, even in the church. The church pews are filled with many broken hearted people due to failed marriages! Yours shall be an exception in Jesus' name.

So, what does adequate preparation for marriage entail? This shall be examined under the following four different segments.

Before You Choose A Marriage Partner

The starting point of adequate preparation for a great marriage is actually during the single years, before you ever get to know, meet or choose your marriage partner.

It begins with self discovery. You need to discover yourself before you try to discover your spouse. Where are you heading for in life? What is your vision, goal, dream, and destination? A proper understanding of this is required because it will determine how and who you choose.

Then, be the best you can be. Deliberately make investment into your own life in all areas. Spiritually, establish a strong spiritual relationship with God through word study and prayer. This will no doubt enhance your spiritual stamina, which will be an advantage to you in building a strong marriage in future. Mentally, develop and be the best you can in your career. This will enhance your worth and not make you a liability to your spouse in future. Be your best emotionally, so you will be able to accommodate a marriage partner in future. Even physically, be the best you can and make yourself fit!

Also, learn as much as you can about marriage. Remember the popular saying, knowledge is power? And the bible says:

> *... a man of knowledge increaseth strength.*
>
> Proverbs 24: 5

Surprisingly, there are married people who have never undertaken any personal study on the subject of marriage, so they grope in the dark, from one form of crisis to another. Many singles who are about to marry, have never read any Christian book on the life – time journey called 'marriage,' which they are about embarking on. So, what do you expect in such marriages? You shall not fail!

The main difference between a marriage that is working and one that is not, is knowledge *(Daniel 11:32; 1 Peter 3:7)*. Learn from credible sources on the subject of marriage. Primarily, study the Bible which is the most credible text on the subject of marriage. You should also study materials – books, magazines, tapes – of people with proven testimonies on the subject.

One of the questions I usually ask singles who inform me of their marriage intention, is whether they have studied any books on the subject of marriage or not. Actually, in our church setting, you are required to have studied a certain number of Christian books on marriage, before you qualify to be wedded in church. I can tell you, this has been very helpful and it will help you a great deal! Study and understand God's provisions for the family, how to run a home and how to relate with in-laws. You could also study biographies of successful couples.

At this stage, it is also important that you pray and believe God for guidance in the correct choice of a right marriage partner when it is time. When you commit your ways unto God in prayer, He will surely direct your path (Psalms 37:4). Remember also that the Bible says if you ask, you will receive because everyone that asks receives (Matthew 7: 7-9). It is wisdom to ask God in prayer in advance, with an open heart, for His choice of a marriage partner.

Personally, ever before I was ready for marriage, God enabled me to spend enough time in prayer, asking for His guidance, choice and perfect will for my life in this regard. In the same vein, for all my children, I spend quality time in prayer, asking God to manifest His perfect will in their lives in this area as well. And, hallelujah, it is working and producing evidence! It will work in your life too. So, don't wait until you are ready for a marriage partner; 'pray in advance', get yourself set and be adequately prepared.

Get busy serving the interest of the kingdom of God, adding value both to your life and those of people around you. Those who seek the Lord are not permitted to lack any good thing – including a covenant marriage partner (Psalms 34:10). Build up yourself sufficiently enough to be able to build a successful marriage without stress. Be a successful individual, whole and distinct! That way, you would be laying a solid foundation for a strong marriage in future.

The Process Of Choosing A Life Partner

This is the second segment. How you choose a marriage partner is usually reflective of your level of preparedness. In exercising your freedom of choice, ensure that you honour the Lord by choosing within the guidelines of His word. It is crucial for you to understand that this is a very crucial process.

Before this time, based on your understanding of scriptures, you ought to have established your own sound principles for living and set up your own boundaries. By the help of the Holy Spirit, establish in advance your values, convictions, perspectives, limits and so on, before another person comes into your world.

If you have all these well laid out, they will inform your choice of a marriage partner. You won't be swinging like a pendulum trying to live by the other person's standards, especially if the standards are negative. If you are well organized and highly principled, it will be difficult if not impossible, to sway you negatively.

The qualities you look out for, while choosing a marriage partner, are a clear indication of your preparedness. Pay more attention to the spiritual matters, which endure rather than just mere feelings or the physical, which are subject to change. Beware of physical yardsticks such as looks, physique, possession, carrier, fame, etc. These are transient and do not guarantee happiness in marriage.

What qualities should I look out for in choosing a marriage partner? You may ask. Well, the following guiding principles will be helpful.

Spiritually: That individual must be a born again and practising Christian. Remember the Bible says:

> *Be ye not unequally yoked together with unbelievers: for what fellowship hath righteousness with unrighteousness? And what communion hath light with darkness?*
>
> *And what concord hath Christ with Belial? Or what part hath he that believeth with an infidel?*

And what agreement hath the temple of God with idols? For ye are the temple of the living God; as God hath said, I will dwell in them, and walk in them; and I will be their God, and they shall be my people.

2 Corinthians 6:14 - 16

The truth is, there is no meeting point between a Christian and an unbeliever, as far as the issue of choosing a life partner is concerned. Never be deceived! It is critically important that both of you have the same spiritual convictions, of major spiritual issues such as: Repentance and salvation, Holy Ghost and water baptism, faith towards God, laying on of hands, resurrection of the dead and eternal judgement (Hebrews 6:1-3).

Knowing and following the will of God is not as complicated as many think, if you truly love Him! Choose someone that has and shows evidence of the fruit of the Spirit (Galatians 5:22- 23). Do not choose a spiritual 'stranger.'

Learn to commit this area of your life, like others to God in prayer and trust Him to guide you. For instance, if you sense a strong attraction that lingers on over a period of time, towards a sister or brother, even when such a person is not around, wisdom demands that you check it out in prayer. Make sure that your spirit is at peace, before you make a move and, don't just ignore uneasiness or unexplainable restlessness in your spirit.

Remember, the Holy Spirit, your indispensable helper is available in matters of this nature. He is a discerner of the thoughts and intents of the heart of man. Engage His help. He alone knows a man's true nature.

Emotional Maturity: Consider such a prospect's stability before you make a choice. Answers to the following sample questions will surely be very helpful: Does such a person have self control? Is he or she mature or under the remote control of family and friends? Is there the ability to adapt and be flexible? How sensitive is he or she to the needs of others? And is there respect for other's perspectives? Does he or she have a balanced, positive and secure self-image?

Mentally: It is important to consider how such a person reasons. How objective is he or she? How about the ability and willingness to communicate? Is he or she ready and willing to make commitments? Do you have similarities in interests, values, education and goals? How responsible is he or she? Remember: responsibility is the price for greatness!

Physical Fitness: Choose someone that you can appreciate, cherish and will not be ashamed to present as your spouse to anyone in future. Pay attention to details, such as the compatibility of your blood genotype. Is he or she gainfully employed?

If you take time to consider these issues in your choice process, it is a great sign of solid preparation for a great tomorrow.

The Courtship Period

In this third segment, we shall examine how your level of preparedness is revealed in the way you handle the period of courtship. What is courtship? You may ask. It is the period between when two people – single and opposite sexes - agree to marry and when they actually do.

Courtship is a necessary part of every successful marriage. It is part of the foundation laying period of marriage. It is no wonder, then that more often than not, the marital trouble that most people go through, is traceable to the fact that their courtship period was not made purposeful.

How do I make courtship period purposeful? You may ask. Good question! Just come along with me as we consider this.

Making Courtship Purposeful

Courtship is not just the time for munching dinner and slurping ice cream together, at a fast food restaurant. It is the period between when two single people of opposite sexes, formally agree to marry and when they actually do. Concerning the birth of Jesus, the Bible says: *'Mary was espoused to Joseph ...* (Matthew 1:18), *a virgin espoused to a man whose name was Joseph ...'* (Luke 1:27). From Matthew 1:18 we also read: *'...before they came together ....'* This actually means that there was a marriage intention between Mary and Joseph; they were in courtship, but they had not yet come together physically.

Courtship can be likened to the seasoning ingredients that you use before preparing a soup. What, when and how you put the ingredients, determine the taste of the soup. Courtship is a time when you both learn to discover more of God together. It is a time when you are left with the responsibility of finding out, with all sincerity, if you truly agree (Amos 3:3).

You have to find out also, what both of you have in common and if both of you have a common vision. It is a time to discover your own pillars that would make your marriage successful. My husband accepted the responsibility and discovered seven pillars, which we both worked upon during our courtship that formed the foundation of the glorious family success we enjoy today.

Our marriage is a testimony of God's goodness, faithfulness, love and power from day one till now. I have never had any cause to regret being married to my husband. I often say, if there is any such thing as *'another life'*, I would still want to be married to my husband again. In heaven, I am sure God has made a provision for my mansion to be next to his.

You can discover yours better, during courtship, by finding out what the word of God says concerning a great marriage. Yours may not necessarily be as many as seven pillars, but there must be something particularly strong in God's word that will easily command His presence in your future home.

One of God's promises concerning marriage says:

> **Whoso findeth a wife findeth a good thing, and obtaineth favour of the Lord.**
>
> Proverbs 18:22

This means that you are at your best when you are married. Marriage promotes; it rewards financially, spiritually, mentally and all round. It also means that being married opens you up to favour with God, which commands favor from everywhere else.

Courtship is your time for good preparation and planning on how, what, where, when and which way you would want your home to be run. Put your faith on the line for a glorious marriage on all issues, including fruitfulness. You can even name your children in advance by faith! Ensure that your confidence in God is in place.

But, if the courtship period is so important, how long should it be? Well, there are no specific scriptural references that say exactly how long it should be. Most Bible examples, vary from couple to couple, like Isaac and Rebecca, Jacob and Rachel, Jacob and Leah in **Genesis 24, 29:1-30**. However, the Word of God says:

> **Wisdom is profitable to direct.**
>
> Ecclesiastes 10:10

Since marriage is a lifetime affair and not a thing to be rushed into, it is important for you to be sure you know each other well enough. Even though courtship is not how long but how well, the period should be reasonably long enough, for both of you to get to know each other well enough, for you to be able to live together all the days of your lives.

My husband and I courted for six years but its effect is speaking now, as it gave me ample time, to know all about what my husband was called into and what to expect in future.

The truth is, you cannot know someone completely, no matter how long you court, but the longer, the better. If you court for only a month or less, then, you will see the effect in your marriage. This is because, knowing each other well, will last almost a lifetime, while learning about each other, will also take time; but you are better off, when you know quite a lot about someone.

A reasonable length of courtship period is a necessity you cannot afford to overlook. In Genesis 29:20-30, Jacob courted Rachel for seven years but was given Leah. Even after that, he still had to court again for another seven years for Rachel! In fact, it was seven years and seven days with Leah's week inclusive.

Personally, I usually recommend minimum, about two years period, before marriage. Why two years? You may ask. Well, life is in seasons; so each year is made up of seasons (Ecclesiastes 3:1). There are four seasons in each year, namely: summer, spring, winter and fall (Genesis 8:22).

Each year, you go through these four seasons, giving you ample opportunity to know each other better. It covers areas such as each one's likes, dislikes, temperaments, past, present as well as future dreams, aspirations and hopes.

Each season comes and goes; maybe not annually as in nature, but it is just as certainly and consistently. This affords you the opportunity to share views, opinions and ideas about various issues. Be open and honest with each other, as this will help you develop genuine friendship and graciousness towards each other.

In two years therefore, you are able to experience each of these four seasons about twice. With this, you are able to make your assurance doubly sure on your choice. Remember the scripture says in the mouth of two or three witnesses the truth may be established (Matthew 18:10). Spend this time to influence each other positively, help each other grow and succeed, develop a winning attitude, deal with past failures and maximize your differences. To make these possible, you must learn to listen empathetically.

So, don't rush into marriage! Look before you leap! Many have rushed into marriage, only to discover the true identity of their spouses when it was already too late.

A lady once came to inform me of her marriage intentions. I wanted to find out some things from her and ask her a few questions. So, I booked an appointment with her.

For some reasons, the appointment could not hold; by the time I met her next, she was already married. The look on her face showed that she needed help. I later discovered that the man she married had been living outside the country for many years and just came back for the wedding. So, they did not really know each other before marriage. She, of course was in a hurry to get married so she could travel back with him.

While there is nothing wrong with a woman wanting to travel with her husband after marriage, there is everything wrong in wanting to marry a man just because you want to go outside the country with him! The man, I guess; knowing his own spiritual limitations, tried to delay the wedding ceremony, but she succeeded in 'convincing' him since she was ready to shoulder all the expenses.

As soon as the wedding ceremony was concluded, she discovered the true nature of the man she had married. He was a man that was never interested in the things of God. She wanted to call it quit, but it was already too late.

If only she had been patient enough, she would have had a better knowledge of the man and most likely would not have gone into that marriage. Now, she has to live the rest of her life in that uncomfortable situation. It can be very dangerous to lack adequate knowledge about someone you are going to spend your life with. This is more dangerous especially in a world that is so technologically advanced that people get married everyday via the internet. It is wise to ensure you know each other well enough before going into marriage.

The benefits of knowing your partner long enough during courtship are innumerable. Some of the benefits both of you stand to gain include: all- round maturity: spiritually, emotionally, physically etc.

This is because of the increased level of understanding of each other that both of you will have, from knowing each other for a long period of time. You will enjoy the benefit of knowing the peculiar characteristics, likes, dislikes, other various weaknesses of each other and know how to handle them (Gen. 5:22-23). You will be able to plan and decide on issues that will affect both of you after marriage such as where to settle after marriage, place of worship, finance, number of children, relationship with family members, vision and other plans that form the important foundation for your future home.

During the courtship period, you must also be fervent and sensitive spiritually. Spend time to pray, fast and study the Bible together. Deepen your knowledge and understanding of the subject of marriage and family by studying and exchanging helpful Christian books, tapes and materials on marriage. Also, you can attend marriage seminars and related special programmes. All these will help to equip you for your future home.

Knowing each other long enough, allows you the benefit of knowing each other's family members such as parents, siblings, close and distant relations. You are able to communicate with them via mails, letters, telephone, etc and generally establish a cordial relationship with them. You can also visit them.

Pay particular attention to how your partner relates with her or his family members. This will go a long way in helping you develop a friendly relationship. It will also help both of you becoming best friends (Proverbs 18: 24).

Finally, knowing each other long enough affords you the opportunity to be able to confidently decide, on whether to marry the person or not. I want to state categorically here that courtship is not equal to marriage: so, it can be broken, if need be.

If while courting, you discover that you made a wrong choice, you are fearful about the future, or that regret getting involved in that relationship and constantly wish you could find a way out of it, or you discover that you both disagree more often than you agree, then wisdom demands that you put a stop to the relationship. All these negative area is a pointer to the fact that you are on the wrong path. Safely make a U-turn as fast as you can! Some have foolishly continued such relationships and ended up in regret.

One couple once came for counsel. They had been

married for about three months then, but were contemplating divorce! After a brief discussion, it was evident that they had been managing and patching vital issues all through the courtship period.

Don't walk on in foolishness, so that you can avoid life-time disaster! How can you see evil and keep going (Proverbs 9:6; 22:3; 20:20)? I want to say categorically here that a broken courtship is not a divorce! However, this should be done in a healthy manner that will glorify God.

I was speaking with a single lady recently. She had come to intimate me with her wedding plans and preparations. It was just a few days before the wedding. In the course of the discussion, it was discovered that the would-be husband had never had any form of communication with any of her relations; neither by mail, letter nor telephone. None of her relations was expected to be present at the wedding ceremony. What do you expect in such a marriage?

Some major characteristics of a good Christian courtship

Watch out for the following necessary things. They will help you to have a correct assessment of your relationship.

Defined destination: Is there a defined destination

that both of you are driving towards in life? Have you both identified your vision and mission on earth and are you moving in that direction or not? To be without a defined destination is like playing football without a goal post! You never score a goal. During courtship, my husband and I already had our destination in life clearly defined. The evidences reflect in our home today, to the glory of God!

Agreement: The bedrock of every marriage is agreement. This begins from the courtship period. Do your discussions usually end in disagreements? Both of you must have agreed to spend the rest of your lives together in marriage. You know, marriage is a lifetime of intimate relationship. So, both of you must be able to agree on crucial issues that concern your future. Remember, two cannot walk together, not even in marriage, except they be agreed (Amos 3:3). Wherever there is no agreement, there will be confusion, disorderliness and disunity. That actually is a workshop for the devil. A healthy agreement helps protect your relationship.

Christian Character: Character is like a smoke. No matter how hard you pretend, it cannot be hidden. You and your partner must have good Christian character traits that speak. Both of you must be God-fearing and doers of God's commandment in truthfulness. You both must be committed to the things of God like fellowship, kingdom service, tithing, offerings etc. This is why God commands that you join yourself with someone of like belief and faith (2 Corinthians 6:14-16). The Christian character of both you and your partner must be such that radiates the fruit of the Spirit mentioned in Ephesians 5:9 and Galatians 5:22. A good Christian character will guide both of you from acting the way unbelievers do, thereby saving you from sorrows and hurts.

Progress: A good Christian courtship should be progressive in nature. This is what makes it healthy. It is a time to prove the relationship. Are you confident that you have made the right decision? Do you experience improvement in your relationship? It should either end up in an engagement and then marriage, or the relationship should be neatly discontinued.

Please note that a courtship if broken does not make it unsuccessful. If you notice stagnation, wisdom demands that you put a stop to that relationship. There should be constant advancement in your relationship during courtship (Proverbs 4:18). There should be progress in every area of life for both of you - physically, spiritually, materially, mentally and in every other area. The success of every good courtship period is that it should end in something even more meaningful.

Pre-Marital Sex: Many begin in the spirit and end up messing themselves up by engaging themselves in the works of the flesh. Galatians 5:19-21 lists the various work of the flesh:

Now the works of the flesh are manifest, which are these; Adultery, fornication, uncleanness, lasciviousness,

Idolatry, witchcraft, hatred, variance, emulations, wrath, strife, seditions, heresies,

Envyings, murders, drunkenness, revellings, and such like: of the which I tell you before, as I have also told you in time past, that they which do such things shall not inherit the kingdom of God.

Since courtship is not marriage, you have no marriage rights over each other's physical body, until marriage has been contracted. Refuse defilement (Hebrews 13:4). When the bed is defiled, the honour in marriage is affected. There is no room for sexual relationship or anything that leads to it, while in courtship. Yes, you intend to marry, but as long as you are not yet married, it is sinful for you to involve yourself in it. Pre-marital sex does not only defile, it also destroys trust, honour and respect. It is like a wound, even when it is healed, the scar still remains.

With the HIV/AIDS scare terrorizing the world today; even the unbelieving and skeptical world has discovered the need for purity. It has suddenly realized that there is no safer precaution than choosing a life of purity and chastity. It is possible to say 'No!' to pre-marital sex. Just choose to seek the Lord uncompromisingly and He will preserve the treasure He created in your bodies. Keep yourself pure!

Preparing For The Wedding Ceremony

This is the fourth and the last segment in this chapter titled: preparing for marriage. The need to be creative in this chapter cannot be over-emphasized here. In preparing for a successful wedding ceremony, certain vital issues and areas need to be given adequate consideration. Let's briefly examine some of them here before this chapter closes.

The Place of Engagement

Engagement is what succeeds a satisfactory courtship period, when both partner have concluded to spend the rest of your lives together in marriage. Let me say clearly here, that an engagement is scriptural and necessary (Genesis 24).

At this time, formal, public introduction of each other is made to certain key people in your lives such as: parents, siblings, pastors, friends, colleagues and relations. Of course, I am aware the procedure differs from culture to culture. In some cultures, it is called traditional wedding. However, irrespective of your culture, it is usually the time of paying the bride price.

Whatever you give as bride price, is supposed to be a demonstration of love, to the relations of your would-be spouse. In Genesis 24:29-60 and Ruth 4:1-12 we see biblical examples of engagement ceremonies.

> *And the servant brought forth jewels of silver, and jewels of gold, and raiment, and gave them to Rebecca: he gave also to her brother and her mother precious things.*
>
> Genesis 24:53

Notice the words *"precious things."* Whatever things that are presented as bride price must be precious; not sinful and not contrary to the word of God. These things ought to be given willingly. Contrary to what some believers think, it is scriptural to pay bride price; however, the things you offer should be precious and not things that will dishonour God or tarnish your Christian testimony.

When my husband and I were about to marry, certain things were included on the list of items that he was to bring as the bride price. We knew that we couldn't be involved in presenting such things and I knew that my husband would rather never be married than present such; because of our Christian faith and our stand for God and our future. Yes, we loved each other and we were looking forward to getting married, but we loved God more.

So, when my husband got the list, he did not respond. We talked over it, prayed about it and we both agreed never to displease God in whatever will be presented as the bride price. Then one day, my father said to him, 'There has been no response from you on the engagement list sent to you.' There and then, with due respect to my dad and with God's wisdom, my husband replied: 'Sir, you see, there were certain things on the list that if we ever get involved in, could make us become problems to you tomorrow; especially because of our Christian faith.'

Immediately, my father also being a practicing Christian agreed and said: "Cancel whatever could be against your faith and future on the list' and that was it! Don't sell your birthright today else you will regret your actions tomorrow!

Since the engagement period, being the peak of the courtship period, both of you should prepare spiritually. Spend more time praying and fasting and gathering knowledge from the word of God concerning His promises and commandments needed for a successful family life. Many couples tend to get carried away with various activities during this period that they never seem to find time for God. If there is any time to seek

God more, it is at this time because this will help both of you to correctly handle any challenges, distractions and contrary reactions during this period.

At this period too, other conclusions such as the materials needed for building a home together, must be reached. This is not the time to start 'hunting' for a job, especially as a man; you should have been productively employed! If you do not have a job, especially as a man, don't even think of marriage yet! You should be prepared enough to embrace the responsibilities that marriage and your future family will demand of you (2 Chronicles 27:6).

Sincerity that is void of every form of pretences is a MUST at this period. Both of you have to be open to each other, hiding nothing from each other and keeping no 'skeletons' in your cupboard. Let your partner know even the tiniest detail about you. I have seen a lot of ladies fall victim to this, simply because they would not let go of 'secrets' and pretences. If for example, you are a lady who likes to wear red lipstick, then don't pretend that you don't wear lipstick at all, only for your husband to stumble on you, wearing one after you are both married. Allow your partner accept you for whom you truly are without assumptions.

During engagement, you obtain the official or public consent of both families and also receive their blessings.

Notice that both Rebekah and Ruth obtained significant and memorable parental and family blessings.

To Rebekah it was said:

And they blessed Rebekah, and said unto her, Thou art our sister, be thou the mother of thousands of millions, and let thy seed possess the gate of those which hate them.

Genesis 24:60

There is no disputing the fact that this has become a reality today. With Abraham, Isaac's father, God made a covenant to make his descendants as the dust of the earth. Rebekah's family without any knowledge of this covenant, pronounced her as the mother of thousands of millions and by her seed, Isaac, this covenant has come to pass.

The same was true of Ruth. The blessings pronounced on her made her the mother of Obed, David's grandfather; the lineage through which Jesus the Messiah came. That's a former gentile now coming into the Messianic lineage of Israel!

And all the people that were in the gate, and the elders, said, We are witnesses. The LORD make the woman that is come into thine house like Rachel and like Leah, which two did build the house of Israel: and do thou worthily in Ephratah, and be famous in Bethlehem:

And let thy house be like the house of Pharez, whom Tamar bare unto Judah, of the seed which the LORD shall give thee of this young woman.

Ruth 4:11-12

So, don't despise parental blessings during engagement and as you prepare for your wedding. If you face any challenges during this period, seek the face of God and believe Him for wisdom on how to handle these successfully.

I must not forget to mention here the need to attend to formalities that are required at the marriage registry (Romans 13:1). This will add all the necessary legal backing to your would-be union.

The Christian Wedding

Marriage should not be a secret deal or a closet thing; it should be before a cloud of witnesses. Nevertheless, you should trust God not to be a burden or a source of concern to your family. Don't make your wedding a Church project - going from one Church member to the other asking for financial assistance. My husband usually says: 'I married by myself, so she is my wife; not a community wife!' That will be your testimony too!

Must The Church Bell Ring?

Having gone through the engagement successfully, don't ever be tempted to overlook the importance of a

Church wedding; that is one of the reasons divorce rate is increasingly high these days. Never subscribe to the norm that a church wedding is unimportant or that marriage can be contracted just anywhere.

For several reasons, a church wedding should be conducted and it is all for your sake, not God's! These reasons include but are not limited to the following.

First, it is scriptural for you to do it. God commands it, and His commandments are not to grieve but to groom you (Matthew 3:15; I John 5:3).

Secondly, a church wedding affords you the singular privilege of having your marriage consummated in the presence of a cloud of witnesses, God being the principal witness. Ordained ministers of the gospel are also present as God's representatives.

Thirdly, you exchange vows; these enhance your commitment to your marriage.

Fourthly, you receive a duly signed church wedding certificate as physical evidence. This you can always use as a point of contact in difficult times, for your desired victory. It is not surprising therefore, that research has proved that most church marriages usually last longer. Many have contacted testimonies by these; you will not be left out!

So, you need a Church wedding where an ordained minister of the gospel, before the congregation of the righteous, pronounces heavens blessings upon you.

> *And the third day there was a marriage in Cana of Galilee; and the mother of Jesus was there:*
>
> *And both Jesus was called, and his disciples, to the marriage.*
>
> John 2:1-2

Remember that Marriage is a covenant relationship between a husband and wife, with God as the third party; while a wedding ceremony is just an event which may probably last one or two days. As long as God is involved, you form a threefold cord that is not easily broken.

> *And if one prevail against him, two shall withstand him; and a threefold cord is not quickly broken.*
>
> Ecclesiastes 4:12

Here are a few tips to help you have a successful church wedding.

Planning: Plan within available resources; not just "by faith." The importance of this cannot be overemphasized. Even the Scriptures agree with this (Luke 14: 28- 32). The phrase: 'Sitteth not down first,' appears twice in this passage; showing the importance of sitting down to plan. God will not plan for you; it is your responsibility to do so and it takes sitting down to plan properly for you to have a successful wedding.

God is a Master planner. Looking at the creation story,

we see that He did not do things haphazardly. He had a plan. He created the seas before the fishes, the earth before man (Genesis 1 & 2). Just imagine what would have happened if He made the fishes before the seas? If you plan properly, you will avoid incurring debts that could affect the well being of your new home. One essential tool that is required for effective planning is wisdom.

> *If the iron be blunt, and he do not whet the edge, then must he put to more strength: but wisdom is profitable to direct.*
>
> Ecclesiastes 10:10

Wisdom will help you make the right choices, know how many guests to invite, how much food to cook, what kind of clothes to buy, how much to spend on the ceremony and so on. Wisdom must be your principal tool if you desire success in that wedding ceremony.

Don't borrow! My husband often says, 'If you can think enough, what you have is enough.' So your problem is not lack of finances but lack of adequate thinking. What you have is enough if you will think enough! Don't borrow for your wedding ceremony, so that you don't become a servant (Proverbs 22: 7). How would you feel when you see the person you borrowed from at your wedding? Very uncomfortable, certainly! Where will be your Christian testimony? Don't you

327

know that your lender will always feel that without him your wedding would never have held? So, instead of God taking all the glory, your lender does!

Whether therefore ye eat, or drink, or whatsoever ye do, do all to the glory of God.

1 Corinthians10:31

All things should be done to the glory of God. There was a couple that borrowed so much for their wedding ceremony that long after the wedding, they were still paying off the debt. It weighed so much on them that you could easily read problems on their faces. When you desire His name to be glorified in all your plans, you will discover that God will take over your wedding – He will surprise you with supplies until your cup runs over. That was exactly what happened during our own wedding over twenty-five (25) years ago! God has not changed; He will do the same thing for you. Borrowing enslaves, don't get entangled in it!

How expensive a wedding is has nothing to do with the success of the marriage. Be modest in your choice of wedding gown, suit, shoes, rings, the reception, cake, food, drinks, photographs, etc. Interestingly, no matter the volume of what you make available, no excess will ever be returned to you after the ceremony! Do not spend all your savings for just one occasion – important as it may be! Determine what you want to spend and try to work within a budget.

Prepare Spiritually: The place of prayer cannot be overlooked. In fact, prayer and planning go hand in hand. The choice of a wedding date for example, requires prayers as well as planning. Prayerfully choose your date and then spend quality time praying about the wedding. You will need to commit every aspect of the event and the service into God's hands.

Even on the wedding day, rather than running helter-skelter, wake up early and spend time with your heavenly Father. You are simply giving Him room to take charge of the day for you. And very importantly, never allow yourself to be stressed out on your wedding day, no matter the pressure! Some are so stressed out that they are worn out, un-coordinated. They even doze during the service and never pay attention to even the message of the day. If there is any message you should never forget in your life, it is the one preached on your wedding day!

Involve Others! While it is true that two alone begin a home, it is also true that a wedding is a social event – it involves members of the society. Can you live alone outside the society? No! So, learn to delegate responsibilities; you cannot do it all alone. Make a list of what needs to be done and identify capable hands that are willing to assist in such areas. Involve other people. Let them know you are getting married and be able to share in the joy of the day with you. Remember, marriage is no secret deal!

After you have fulfilled all righteousness (Matthew 3:11) and the marriage has been duly consummated, you are then publicly pronounced as husband and wife! The future becomes yours for the taking.

As you take heed to these, marital success becomes your portion, in Jesus name!

A Word of Hope

In case you got married as unbelievers and for some reason you did not formally contract your union – either by paying the bride price, conducting the court or Church wedding; perhaps you just 'moved in' and have been living together ever since, whatever your case may be: all hope is not lost!

Go and make necessary amends: pay the bride price, go to the registry, ask for pastoral blessing and block all covenant leakages. Haven't you heard of instances where the man died and the woman who had lived with him all those years is kicked out by her in-laws? I am aware of instances where all properties and belongings were taken away and both the woman and her children were left with nothing. In some cases such action comes because of the lack of legal backing in the marriage. In some other cases, the acts are due to acts of wickedness from relations. You will succeed!

Chapter 15

It Happened to me

For I know the thoughts that I think towards you, saith the Lord, thoughts of peace, and not of evil, to give you an expected end.

Jeremiah 29:11

God's thoughts towards you continually are that of peace. He never desires to put you in any situation that does not guarantee your peace. So, anytime you find yourself in any situation or circumstance where His thoughts of peace are not finding expression, know that the enemy is at work. My husband often says: 'If it is not good, it is not God.'

In such situations, one of the key weapons you need to engage is that of testimonies. The Bible says:

The thing that hath been, it is that which shall be; and that which is done is that which shall be done: and there is no new thing under the sun.

Ecclesiastes 1:9

No matter the situation you find yourself in right

now, it is not new! It has happened before and it is not peculiar to you. So, don't look at your circumstances and conclude that your case is negatively different. Anything that is not good, whatever it may be, has only one source: the devil. So, fight him with the weapon of testimonies!

The Bible says in Revelation 12:11,

> *And they overcame him by the blood of the Lamb, and by the word of their testimony; and they loved not their lives unto the death.*

You can be a testimony; your life can become a positive reference point. After waiting, preparing for a great future in grand style, having maximized your single years, making a difference via knowledge and by the help of the Holy Spirit; you deserve to be a celebrity; you can be a testimony.

What are testimonies?

Testimonies are faith boosters. They are truth; they are not only true but the truth. They are the righteous acts of God, the proofs that God is still at work on earth today. We can engage testimonies the same way we engage scriptures in becoming what God's plan is for us.

Testimonies help you to generate faith and destroy doubts. In other words, every time you hear or read a testimony, your faith mounts up! You are stirred up in your spirit to believe that God is still at work in your case too.

As you believe what you read about others and key into them, you have already put the devil to shame because when you believe it and declare it, God is committed to perform it for you. You will not miss your portion in Jesus name.

Testimonies also help to fortify your confidence in God, so that you are able to approach the throne of grace with boldness (Hebrew 4:16). Hezekiah put God to remembrance (Isaiah 38: 3) and he was justified. God had to send Isaiah back to revert what He had earlier said. The Bible says:

> *Put me in remembrance: let us plead together: declare thou, that thou mayest be justified.*

Isaiah 43:26

You can put God in remembrance by testimonies. He is the same yesterday, today and forever (Hebrews 13:8), He is no respecter of persons (Acts 10:34-35) and He is rich unto all that call upon Him (Romans 10:12). What He did for one, He can reproduce in your own life also. So, you can take testimonies to Him in prayers and be guaranteed divine intervention in your situation.

Testimonies will lead to the rejoicing of your heart, because they authenticate the reality of God.

Thy testimonies have I taken as an heritage for ever:
for they are the rejoicing of my heart.

Psalm119: 111

Perhaps, you may have been troubled because things have not been working the way you planned; when you remember how God did it for somebody else, you are encouraged and you begin to rejoice and in your rejoicing, God steps in to deliver your own into your hands because, the Bible says: *"Therefore with joy shall ye draw water out of the wells of salvation"* (Isaiah 12:3). That is how it works, and I see it work for you!

Testimonies are also prophetic. *"… For the testimony of Jesus is the spirit of prophecy"* (Revelations 19:10). Every testimony in this chapter is a pointer that God cannot lie. He has reserved your own miracles because it shall be duly duplicated.

I want you to know however, that being positively different is not a function of beauty, career, possession, or any such thing, but of the favour of God. Whatever you want to become: fulfill destiny, enjoy divine health, live without stress, be gainfully employed, etc.; all you need is to believe God for His favour and He will not deny you.

Read carefully the following amazing testimonies of some singles that were positively different in various life endeavors and meditate on them. As you do, I see God rid your life of every form of shame. You plug into these testimonies by believing them. Do warfare with them and they shall be reproduced in your life. These testimonies will surely kindle your hope and the effect shall be seen by all and sundry.

See What The Lord Has Done!

Changed via knowledge

I am not yet married. I am single but in courtship. I have been following your teachings on 'Family matters' over the internet and I'm so grateful for the great knowledge you have given me. I am changed and so is my courtship.

— FAVOUR, N

I can see my happy future.

I am a young lady of twenty four and not married. I have been reading your article online and I have been really blessed. I'm learning to be the kind of lady God wants me to be and I have begun to foresee my forever happy and blessed marriage before I even say 'I do.'

— TABBY, N.

Integrity pays

I scored 262 in the just released UME results. I have never passed it before by myself because someone always helps me to write the examinations, which I know is not right. But now, I wrote it myself and passed and I believe that God is real and it pays to be honest.

— *LEKAN, P.*

11 Years Spinsterhood Destroyed

I had believed God for a life partner for 11 years before I joined this commission in the year 2000. Then, my pastor used to tell us that if you belong to this commission for four years without a testimony, it is your fault. I keyed into it and whole heartedly, I gave my life to Christ.

In May 2002, which was the 21st anniversary of the ministry, our pastor stressed on divine release and divine restoration I keyed into it and by June 2002, my husband appeared that was a confirmation of the word of the servant of God in Shiloh 2003 to everyone believing to be married. I got married and nine months after, God blessed us with a baby boy.

— *OKWUFIA, J*

Destiny Opened

I discovered in my life that everything I started never had an end. I did not finish my secondary school education, I tried to pursue cosmetology course but I could not finish. I had never obtained a certificate in my life. But I gave my life to Jesus and for the first time in my life I was baptized and was given a baptismal *certificate. Praise God*

Now Financially Relevant

The Lord changed my story! I heard the testimony of someone that God increased because he paid his tithe and offering, so I keyed into it. I calculated my tithe based on where I am now to what 125% increase would be. And I told God that all through this year, I would be paying the amount, no matter how difficult it would be. I located some scriptures, which I read every morning.

After about a week, I was called for a chat in one of the multinational companies that have an office in Nigeria. I attended, with my faith intact. God intervened! The lady that was supposed to be my immediate boss took it upon herself as if I was her candidate.

Later, I was called for essay test. The following Friday, I was called upon to collect my appointment letter. And the Lord has surpassed my 125% increase.

Secondly, I came to Lagos last year from Port Harcourt. When I was leaving, I gave out my apartment to a sister free and I believed that when I got to Lagos I would not be running from one post to the other to go to work; my house would be close to my place of work. It came to pass, God gave me accommodation that is actually paid for in dollars and I did not pay a dime. I just moved in, I practically walk to work. And God has also given me a

338

piece of land. I just want to give Him all the glory.

— UCHECHUKWU, M

Job, Marriage, Lifting

I came here for Shiloh, desperate. I looked at my life, everything was stagnated. There was no job, I was struggling and my parents couldn't support me. So, I made up my mind to come and meet God at Shiloh 2004. After the prophetic utterances, January 2005, I got a job with an oil and gas servicing company in the accounting department.

In that same Shiloh Papa declared there would be explosion of marriages. As at that time, I wasn't married. That time, I just keyed into that word and I saw myself realizing it. On November 26th 2005I got wedded.

I came for Shiloh 2005 with my wife, believing God for change Beloved, in July 2006; God told me that I was going to be an export broker. So, I created a web site showcasing what is produce-able in Nigeria.

On the 14th day of last month, I was in my usual duty post; God gave me an appointment letter as a sea engineer in an oil and gas servicing company. That was the post of a full engineer with a salary of 1million naira just for a start. I just want to appreciate God for everything. For seven days I was just looking at the letter because I didn't know what to do. Help me thank God.

— NWACHUKWU, R.

Double Blessing

Praise the Lord; I'm from the Sanctuary Keeper's Group of the church here in Faith Tabernacle, Ota. God has been faithful. I came to Shiloh last year, I had no job; I was also believing God for a husband. And during the pre-Shiloh encounter, God visited me. Before the end of December, the Lord brought a man in my life. The Lord also gave me a miracle job. I assumed duties on February 5th and six weeks later was promoted. This week Wednesday I was again promoted three steps ahead. Praise the Lord.

— EBIYOMI, C

Now Happy and Fulfilled

I joined this commission for the purpose of seeking a husband. However, I started hearing the true word of God to the extent that I almost forgot what I came here for. On one Sunday, the Bishop ministered on Matthew 6:33, "But seek ye first the kingdom of God and all these things shall be added unto you". It dawned on me that all things referred to in that scripture include a husband. At that time, I was 45 years old. Subsequently, I started seeking God, I looked unto Him and I told myself it was my turn. Again, as if Bishop knew what was on my mind, he said "ask for 24hrs miracle". I said God, if all things are possible with you then, my getting married is possible. Miraculously, that same Sunday, I came in contact with

340

my husband! We got married six months later. I can say that I am now happy and fulfilled.

*— **WILLIAMS, P***

Divine Connection!

I joined this commission in 2005 after my National Youth Service (NYSC). The first statement I heard from the Bishop when I stepped in here was: "this is your turning point; this is your place of turning point". I claimed those words. The following month I received a text message asking me to come for a written test in one of the multinational companies. During my preparations, I was trying to connect my friends if they could help me before the interview but all ended in frustration. But the Holy Spirit led me to a particular material which I studied for the interview. When I got to the test centre, that was exactly what came out: I was dazed.

My colleagues were 'sweating' in the exam hall; within five minutes I'd already finished. During the second stage of the interview, the Holy Spirit helped me; I was able to answer all their questions. They asked me to come for the final stage which I did. At the end of the interview I knew I shall not be denied. When I got home, I read in Acts 16:25 how Paul and Silas prayed at midnight. At midnight on Wednesday, I was praying and singing praises to God. When I woke up the following day the first call I received was that I should come and pick up my employment letter. Now, I have been made a manager. The package is indeed glorious. Hallelujah.

— NWOSE, R

No More Age Barrier

I graduated in the year 2002, and ever since then every attempt to move forward has been a challenge. The last one I had was last year, I was said to be over-aged. I was advised to have an "official age' different from my true age; since that is what most people do. But I declined. God knows my age and I cannot lie about it. Then from there God led me and I started writing ICAN professional exams. Out of over 30,000 candidates that participated in the whole of Nigeria, only 206 qualified; that is below one percent: and I'm one of them. I give God the praise.

Also, God endowed me with grace and between then and now I have written five books which have been published.

— KOSOKO, A

Gainfully Employed

For two years, I was jobless, professionally. The declaration for the month of March says: 'arise, prayer changes things'. I keyed into it and two years joblessness was broken. Precisely on 15th of March 2007, during one of our choir rehearsals our leader told us that if you serve God sincerely from your heart and God does not reward you, you should leave the choir. I keyed into that. Miraculously, that very week, I was called to take up an appointment with one of the oil companies, as a sales executive. The third week of March, to the glory of God; I got another job as a cargo surveying engineer. Praise God.

— *JOHN, M.F*

Totally Healed

Since I joined this commission, my eyes have been open to the mystery of the communion, anointing and washing of feet. For twenty years, I have been suffering from hyenia. I have gone to different hospitals, where I was given drugs but no positive result.

But when I became knowledgeable about what it means to believe in the mysteries, I began applying them daily. Then in the month of 'total health is my heritage', the Bishop taught us what it takes for someone to be a lion spiritually; the differences between a sheep and a lion spiritually. My understanding was opened and I saw myself as a spiritual lion. I knew within me that I was going to get my miracle. I decided against every form of distraction and focused my attention on everything happening on the altar.

Immediately, there was as it were a fire in my body; I felt like going to the ladies but I resisted it because I didn't want to be distracted. Today to the glory of God: no more ulcer, no more hyenia; they have all disappeared! Now, I can eat whatever my mates eat. No more pains!

— *EJIOFOR, N*

Lost Job Restored After Paying Tithe

In the year 2000, before I joined this commission, I lost my job. By the year 2002, I joined this commission and came to Shiloh. I made a vow to God that if I get a job I was going to do something for Him. By the year 2004 I decided to pay my entire tithe from the very day I joined this church. One month later, I got a miracle job and by July last year, my former employer called me back and paid me all my arrears from year 2000 till this very time. It was over five million (5,000,000) naira! I was also promoted as Senior Lecturer and back dated to 2000. Again I am expecting money. I give God praise.

— *RICHARDS, A.*

Healed Of Ulcer

I came to this ground with a stomach ulcer and when Mama mounted the pulpit on Wednesday teaching on healing, I keyed into her word and without medication decided to participate in the fasting and prayer exercise. Meanwhile if it were before, I would feel some pains; but now I am healthy and sound, healed of ulcer. I give God all the glory.

— *CHRISTIAN, A.*

Favour

I have been struggling since the age of 14 on my own. Miraculously, God took me to Abuja and gave me a presidential connection. I am staying in the State house presently. Also, I got a miraculous admission to the University of Abuja; which I never sweated for. Now, God has fulfilled the desires of my heart.

— AYODELE, A.

Destiny Restored!

I am a broadcaster by profession and a member of the Press and Publicity Unit of the Church. Before I joined this Commission, I was having a difficult time in my profession. It was very terrible. So, when I became a member, I asked God to distinguish me. In the year 2001, I had an encounter with God which led to breakthroughs on every side.

Two (2) years later, things started going bad again. I then told God that I have entered into a commission where I can not get down anymore.

I decided to attend the Word Of Faith Bible Institute (WOFBI) where I received knowledge. And after WOFBI, I noticed that things became a little bit better. I started my own independent media outfit. It was not easy at the initial stage but the God of this commission proved Himself; the summary of all I'm saying is that right now, the Lord has restored me! There is a T.V. programme called 'Rejoice Africa', which I present and the produce. I have my own outfit and now I have four people working for me. To God be all the glory.

— **PETER, W**

250 Percent Increase

I got to a point where I was tired of the way things were going in my life. I desired a solution and I made up my mind and applied for three weeks leave from my office in order to attend WOFBI, June special. Throughout this period I was alone with God. I did not feel like hearing any other person's voice except my God. To the glory of God, throughout those three weeks everything began to change including my walk with God.

The first week when I got back to the office, my boss called me with the proposal to send me to Benin to represent the company. I was then promoted and within six months, everything worked out smoothly. I desired again for a bigger job, and I vowed my first salary as an offering to God. A month later, a top bank in the country invited me for an interview and to the glory of God I will assume duties there tomorrow.

— **MFON, E**.

Married Against All Odds!

I started believing God for a wife in 1990. When I came

to this church, I joined the Sanctuary Keepers' Unit and told the Lord, 'Whatever is blocking my blessings, as I am cleaning your sanctuary, clear all those things away from my life.'

At a service, Bishop Oyedepo made an altar call for those who believed God for a partner. I went out, and we were prayed for. Before then, everybody in my group referred to me as 'the unrepentant bachelor,' as I was already 40 years old and had had four different broken courtships. To God be the glory, I got married against all odds.

— *OSEMOYA, R*

Total Restoration!

Two days to Shiloh 2003, I was jilted and I came to Shiloh with that burden. I prayed to God that I would want to come with my husband the next Shiloh. When Mama (Pastor Faith Oyedepo) came to preach, she said marriage was not the source of joy but God. I decided to be happy with my God by putting the past behind and totally follow God as well as to continue my life. In the year 2004, God located my husband and in March we got married and in April 2006 we had our baby girl. I give all the Glory to God.

— *OBAJAJA, A*

You Are Next In Line!

You have gone through these testimonies as proofs

of the efficacy of the word of God in the lives of others. Be assured that God is no respecter of persons.

The Bible says:

> *For there is no difference between the Jew and the Greek: for the same Lord over all is rich unto all that call upon him.*
>
> Romans 10:12

Your present circumstance and situation not withstanding; if you put God's word as examined in this book to work, your life will become a living proof of God's faithfulness that cannot fail. Remember:

> *But be ye doers of the word, and not hearers only, deceiving your own selves.*
>
> James 1:22

Your story will definitely change for the better and you too will be able to say: **'It happened to me!'**

SINNERS PRAYER

You have read this book with understanding and you desire to come out, as an envy of the world, a man and a woman that will be noted for distinction.

But the truth is that you cannot be different from others that are facing single life challenges without solutions, if you do not belong to Him who can give you solutions to the problems and temptations of life.

The Bible makes it clear that there is no temptation that you might be facing now that is uncommon, and God has already made a way of escape (I Corinthians 13:10). That singular way is that you give your life to Jesus Christ and be born again.

If you are yet to give your life to Jesus you need to take this all-important step as stated in the word of God says:

"That if thou shalt confess with thy mouth the Lord Jesus, and shalt believe in thine heart that God hath raised him from the dead, thou shalt be saved. For with the heart man believeth unto righteousness; and with the mouth confession is made unto salvation."

Romans 10:9-10

You therefore need to confess your sins and repent from them. Ask Jesus to come into your heart by saying this prayer out loud:

Lord Jesus, I acknowledge that I am a sinner who has come short of your glory. But your Word says, if any man shall call upon you such a one shall be saved.

I therefore call on you today to save me. I believe that Jesus died for me on the cross at Calvary; His blood has the power to wash away my sins.

On the third day He rose again so that I can be justified. Now I confess, you are the lord of my life, deliver me from every form of unrighteousness and write my name in the book of life. Thank you Lord, for now I know that I am born again Amen.

Congratulations!

Now you are born again, you have a new life in Christ. Welcome to a life of exploit as a single, making a difference from henceforth!

ABOUT THE AUTHOR

FAITH ABIOLA OYEDEPO HAS BROUGHT HOPE, JOY, AND LIFE INTO MANY HOMES IN HER GENERATION.

Having received a ministry for family and homes, she has dedicated her life to showing people God's perfect will for their homes and family relationships. Her weekly newspaper and internet columns: Family Matters, Family Success and Family Life have helped in no small way in achieving this goal.

She has shown in practical terms and through deep spiritual insight that the home can be the Eden God created it to be.

She has a divine mandate to make her shoulders available and enrich the lives of singles in a unique way.

Pastor Faith has written more than 12 books, including: Marriage Covenant, Making Marriage Work, Raising Godly Children, and her best selling title: Rescued From Destruction.

An anointed preacher of the gospel, Pastor Faith Abiola Oyedepo has been doggedly supportive of her husband (Dr. David o. Oyedepo, the Visioner and President of Living Faith Church Worldwide Inc.) in the daunting work of the ministry.

She has four children – David Jnr., Isaac, Love and Joys.

Books Authored by Faith A. Oyedepo

The Effective Minister's Wife

Single With A Difference

Rescued From Destruction

Making Marriage Work

Marriage Covenant

Raising Godly Children

You Can Overcome Anxiety

The Dignity Of The Believer

A Living Witness

Communion Table

Nurturing The Incorruptible Seed

Service: The Master Key

Stirring Up The Grace Of God

Building A Successful Family

The Spirit of Faith

Visit our website for weekly articles
by the author:
http://www.davidoyedepoministries.org